D0034536

MVFOL

Fresenius Medical Care North America
2010 Clinical Managers Conference

IT'S OUR SHIP

Also by Captain D. Michael Abrashoff

It's Your Ship
Get Your Ship Together

IT'S OUR SHIP

The No-Nonsense Guide to Leadership

CAPTAIN D. MICHAEL ABRASHOFF

**BUSINESS
PLUS**

NEW YORK BOSTON

Business Plus
Hachette Book Group USA
237 Park Avenue
New York, NY 10017
Visit our Web site at www.HachetteBookGroupUSA.com.

Business Plus is an imprint of Grand Central Publishing.
The Business Plus name and logo are trademarks of Hachette Book Group USA, Inc.

Printed in the United States of America

First Edition: May 2008

10 9 8 7 6 5 4 3 2 1

Library of Congress Cataloging-in-Publication Data
Abrashoff, D. Michael.
  It's our ship : the no-nonsense guide to leadership / Captain D. Michael Abrashoff — 1st ed.
    p. cm.
  ISBN-13: 978-0-446-19966-7
  ISBN-10: 0-446-19966-4
  1. Leadership—United States. 2. Management. 3. Command of troops. 4. United States.
Navy—Management. 5. United States. Navy—Personnel management. I. Title.

  VB203.A638 2008
  658.4'092—dc22

                                                                        2008000497

To our men and women in uniform,
who are serving to protect our freedom.

Contents

IT'S OUR SHIP

INTRODUCTION

Satchel Paige, the legendary major league pitcher, was famous for cautionary maxims. He urged people to shun running at all times, to "go very light on the vices," and to "avoid fried meats, which angry up the blood." And everyone smiles at this tip: "Don't look back. Something might be gaining on you." But Satchel had it slightly wrong. I've found that the more I look back, the smarter I am about the present. And that, in a nutshell, is what this book is about: the unimagined lessons I've been privileged to learn in the six years since I wrote my first book, *It's Your Ship*.

That book described how my crew and I turned a high-tech but dysfunctional guided-missile destroyer, USS *Benfold*, into the best damn ship in the Navy. The book became a best-seller on the business lists, and when I left the service in 2001, it launched me into a new career on the lecture circuit. I spend most of my time speaking to business leaders, helping them apply my *Benfold* experience to the challenges they face today. I now make about a hundred speeches a year.

I am writing again because it turns out that *It's Your Ship* was only a beginning. And now I've found my own Satchel-ism: The past is gaining on me and shedding new light on the present.

I was a relatively young man when I left the Navy, just forty, and my education was a work in progress. It still is. The leaders I speak to have much to say in return, and I listen and learn. I also spend time thinking about my Navy experience, comparing it to the real-life conditions my audiences meet head-on every day. I've made a point of staying in touch with many of the 310 men and women who served with me on *Benfold*, and their memories have become a new source of learning for me. As a result, my message has changed somewhat.

The biggest shift is reflected in the one-letter difference between the title of this book and the title of my first one: I now know that it has to be "our" ship, not "your" ship. As a young commanding officer fighting to make my mark in the Navy, I was a bit too self-centered. Determined to go beyond standard performance and make my ship outstanding, I understood that the only way I could do that was by enlisting the whole crew in the cause. I had to make them take ownership of the ship and its mission, and persuade them to cooperate and work together rather than compete with one another in watertight compartments. I tried to put myself in the shoes of both my crew members and my customer, the battle group commander, and I strove to anticipate the commander's needs before he even knew he had them.

My approach worked, and together we made *Benfold* the go-to ship in the Pacific Fleet, the first ship the admiral thought of when he had a tough assignment. We were the star ship, winning the prestigious Spokane Trophy in 1997 as the most combat-ready ship in the whole Pacific Fleet. But my big mistake was never putting myself in the shoes of my peers, my fellow captains. Had I done so, I would have recognized *Benfold* as a ship that had become a little too cocky and arrogant amid all the praise. The other captains weren't hoping, as I imagined they were, to make their ships match *Benfold*; some of them hoped we would run aground.

I figured out that my own people had to work together as a team to improve the ship, but I failed to take that insight to the next level, where I would have seen *Benfold* as one ship in a ten-ship battle group. Because of my shortsightedness, I never did one thing to help another ship in the group in the two years I spent as *Benfold*'s commander. In fact, I took a great deal of pleasure whenever we bested the performance of any of our group mates. In hindsight, I readily admit that my sights were locked on my own ambition, to the detriment of the larger mission. I wasn't mature enough or smart enough to recognize that if one of the other ships in the group fell down on the job and caused the aircraft carrier to sink, the whole battle group would fail. In that event, it wouldn't matter that *Benfold* was the best ship.

So, with the benefit of time and my exposure to the experiences of others, I now have a revised message: I would now say to every man and woman aboard, "It's not *your* ship; it's *our* ship." It's a vessel that belongs to and depends on every member of the crew, and it is also part of a fleet of ships with a larger mission that the whole crew must own. Thanks to the thousands of men and women who have made up my audiences these past seven years, I have come to understand that my principles and techniques can succeed to their fullest extent only if all involved take ownership for the wider mission. I've had to rethink some of those principles and techniques, and I've come across some new ones that I never imagined in the *Benfold* days.

In the chapters ahead, I've set a course that I believe will help any leader and his or her crew make the voyage from great dreams to great success. Along the route are benchmarks that must be met to ensure progress. Each chapter describes key skills of a good leader and distills those skills into a set of lessons that bring together what I've learned from life and other leaders.

Here's a quick preview of the chapter topics along with a summary of the main points:

• Getting people started off on the right foot and keeping them striding confidently forward is crucial to any successful venture. Frosty welcomes make new crew members unnecessarily wary of the jobs they should be eager to begin. And their trepidation is likely to slow the mission itself. Chapter 1 shows leaders how to attract the right kind of people, how to bring them aboard in a warm and welcoming fashion, and how to keep them happy and eager to come to work every day.

• Excellence has always defined winning organizations. But even perfectly nice, basically competent people may be stumped as to what your company means by excellence and how they must achieve it. Chapter 2 suggests ways you can show your crew members what excellence on the job is all about, and then inspire them to reach for the stars themselves. You can vastly speed your efforts by sharing responsibility for decision making, building confidence through training, instilling respect for even the lowliest job, and giving everyone a stake in the organization's success. The sooner you make it "our" ship, the sooner you and your crew will be cruising at flank speed.

• Truth-tellers may be applauded in theory, but when a bad-news bearer shows up in real life, far too many leaders shoot first and ask questions later (if they ask at all). Let's face it, some harried executives prefer "aye-aye" men and women, even when it's in their best interest to hear the worst. But leaders have enormous incentive to encourage truth-telling. Chapter 3 shows how: Applaud candor even when it hurts; keep your preferences to yourself to prevent suck-ups from parroting them back to you; set an example for your crew by publicly delivering bad news to a superior without delay; and privately challenge questionable decisions from on high (diplomatically, of course).

• A careless leader can wreak havoc on an organization, destroying unity and disgusting employees to the point where they start hiding from the turmoil, biding their time till they can escape to another job. Soon collaboration vanishes, people bicker, sabotage begins, and the workplace is totally dysfunctional. Chapter 4 describes how to bring people together as a high-performance unit primed for success. Vital steps forward include discouraging mindless rivalry, making collaboration a top priority, setting high standards, doing whatever you can to make the job fun, and being generous with your praise.

• "Trust but verify," Ronald Reagan was fond of saying. I say verify trust by outlawing devious, inconsistent, manipulative, and self-serving behavior in the managerial ranks. A leader whose focus is fastened firmly on his own ambitions will be seen—and rightly so—as untrustworthy by his subordinates. They know instinctively that he won't think twice about sacrificing their best interests in pursuit of his own. Chapter 5 explains how to create a climate of trust—the only atmosphere in which your team can become its best, most productive self. Among my suggestions: Show your people that you put them first; keep your promises or explain why you can't; treat your people with respect; and delegate authority.

• Mixed signals and confusing instructions are no way to inspire excellence. In today's high-speed global economy, fuzzy words, like fuzzy accounting, can kill your business. Clarity is the key to infusing your workplace with meaning and purpose. Chapter 6 describes the methods I used in the Navy to get my sailors rowing in the same direction: Inspire all hands by recounting your company's previous achievements; clearly state your ethical guidelines; make sure everyone understands why a job is necessary; stress your core values; avoid diversions and focus on what truly matters.

• Risk is unavoidable in rich lives and thriving businesses. Recklessness is not only optional, it's stupid. The best leaders calculate their odds of success and minimize risks by plotting Plan B, an alternate route ensuring access if the preferred way is blocked. Chapter 7 will navigate you through any sea of risk. It shows how to hedge your bets, steer clear of risks that aren't really worth taking, and recognize when the payoff for accepting risk is just too big to ignore.

• "Leading by example" may be a cliché, but if you don't exemplify what you want people to do, they won't do it. Leaders really have no choice. When you take charge, people watch you closely for signs of what you believe, who you truly are, and what expectations you have for them. Chapter 8 offers my advice for turning their constant scrutiny into teachable moments. Your failures, for example, can be turned into powerful lessons for those who would be your students. Also, the best teachers are those who unselfishly ignore their own interests while setting their people up to succeed. And last but by no means least, the best example a good leader can give boils down to four simple words: Do the right thing.

Some of the material in *It's Our Ship* is drawn from my experiences with former officers and sailors. But the chapters ahead analyze the subtle changes I am now able to discern in a leader's role, whether it be in unifying and motivating a crew or leading by example and choosing the right risks to take.

In the intervening years, I've also broadened my view of the prize open to anyone willing to do what it takes to work at full potential, take ownership of the job, and become the go-to person, the one the boss picks first for the most important assignments. The payoff is far more important than praise, pride, promotion, and a measure of control over the way you spend your days. Working to full potential allows you to master your own destiny—the prize most worth shooting for.

In that great game, you compete against many forces but, above all, against yourself. At the Naval Academy, I had an undistinguished academic record. I was mostly an A student who was content with C's. I even had one professor who told me that I would never make it as a naval officer. Once I graduated, I busted a gut working hard to prove to myself that he was wrong. I worked longer hours than anyone else and was driven to get better results than anyone else. In retrospect, I was competing against myself, not my peers.

As I prepared to take command of USS *Benfold* for the first time, I started thinking about the bigger picture and realized that I wanted more than just to compete against myself. I wanted to leave a legacy. I thought about my role models, one of whom was the ship's namesake, Edward C. Benfold. He was a medic in the Korean War. One afternoon, when he was tending to two wounded marines, their foxhole was stormed by enemy soldiers tossing grenades. Benfold picked up those grenades and charged the incoming soldiers, blowing up them and himself but saving the lives of the two marines.

When I took command of his ship, I wanted to lead his crew with the honor, courage, and integrity with which he gave his life. I also wanted Edward Benfold always to be proud of his ship. That's why my crew and I always tried to do the right thing.

My other role model was my father, a World War II veteran. As I took command of *Benfold*, I realized that I would have to work hard to match the wonderful example of compassion and excellence he had shown my brother, my sisters, and me. I knew much was expected of me if I were ever to fill his shoes. Four months before he passed away in 2003, his feet were hurting him so I bought him a new pair of shoes. After he died, I asked my mother if I could have them back. I still wear those shoes and will keep them always.

As you read this book and think about your own leadership journey, take a hard look at the legacy you are creating and ask yourself if anyone would want to fill your shoes. Ahead lie the stories of other legacy seekers and how they tried to take command of their own destinies.

CHAPTER I

AHOY!

WELCOME ABOARD OUR SHIP

OLD SALTS GIVE SHIPS HUMAN TRAITS, USUALLY FEM-inine, so I am positive that *Benfold* was the most beautiful destroyer in the United States Navy. I never tired of returning from shore to board her spectacular hull, as if meeting her for the first time. I could almost see her smiling and murmuring, "Welcome aboard." I am fantasizing, yes, but then my reverie is often interrupted by memories of a very different ship—my first—and how completely unwelcome that ugly bucket made me feel at all times in all ports. There were times when I actually felt ill at the thought of having to go back to her.

My introduction to the rusty frigate USS *Albert David* was a brush-off—the total opposite of how to greet an aspiring acolyte. It was a dreary, rainy day in San Diego, as bleak as January gets when the Pacific churns up a winter storm. There I stood on the quarterdeck, waiting for anyone to notice my arrival. I was a new ensign, fresh from the U.S. Naval Academy. I yearned to do everything right, but already felt in the wrong.

As I had been taught at Annapolis, I had written to the captain as soon as I received the assignment, introducing myself and asking what my duty would be. This is a hallowed Navy tradition. My classmates all got cordial replies from their new commanding officers, but I hadn't heard a word. Soon I wondered whether I'd had the right address, whether the letter had gotten lost in the mail, whether I should send another—aimless, useless fretting. As weeks became months, I worried that I might have said something inappropriate and alienated my new commanding officer.

Now, months later, here I was reporting aboard my frigate, and no one seemed to know or care.

After what must have been half an hour, the officer I was replacing finally turned up to show me around the ship. He hated the Navy and was miserable and not shy about sharing his frustrations with anyone. I met all the other officers except the captain. What a green officer should be told about the ship he would serve on had apparently escaped them. All I heard was complaining about the "challenges" the ship faced. My initiation to *Albert David* was haphazard, to say the least. I had reported with high enthusiasm; now my concern became dread.

Then I met the captain. When I asked if he had gotten my letter, he said, "Yeah, I have it here in my in-basket." He had read it but hadn't bothered to respond—so much for all my agonizing. Now he told me that I would be the ship's communications officer and that I was inheriting a mess. Talk about a heart-sinking welcome for a new officer. Nevertheless, the captain seemed pleasant enough, at least in port. When we got to sea, he turned out to be what we all considered a tyrant, an officer who yelled at people until pulsating veins popped up on his head and neck. To me, the tension on the ship was palpable, and I had to live in that charged, ulcer-producing climate for twenty-seven months.

The only bright spot in my entire first day came when I met my chief petty officer (CPO), Bob Dooley, who had reported to the ship two weeks before me. Chief petty officers are responsible for training young officers, teaching them the practical facts they never learned in the Naval Academy and how to behave in real-world situations. Navy lore has it that a chief petty officer can make or break a new division officer. Thanks to Chief Dooley, I made it through my first assignment and went on to a successful career in the Navy.

When I asked him how he wanted us to work together, he said, "You stay out of the business down here. I'll take care of you. You get your qualifications and learn how to drive this ship [at Annapolis, I had chosen to become a ship driver] and represent us well up there." That was the beginning of a great relationship between the chief and me. I could confide anything to him, knowing it would go no further.

Chief Dooley and I were responsible for all communications to and from the ship, and we read all of the commodore's personal messages, called P4s (personal for), whenever he was onboard. Once, when an irate commanding officer sent the commodore an inappropriate P4, the chief took the opportunity to impart sound advice. He took me aside and told me, "Now, whenever you're upset, write your message and then put it in your in-basket. If you still feel the same way forty-eight hours later, send it. But if you've calmed down and it might make you look childish, tear it up." Following that bit of wisdom has saved me many an embarrassing moment.

It was also Chief Dooley who first taught me one of my most important leadership lessons: Put yourself in the boss's shoes and analyze what he thinks and does to prepare yourself to do his job. We became a great team, and I loved every minute of working with him. He never once let me down, and I learned more from Bob Dooley about how to be an officer than I ever did from my fellow officers.

This chapter draws an entire cargo hold of lessons from my unwelcoming arrival aboard poor old *Albert David* and my subsequent recovery from feeling sunk before even leaving port. Applicable to all hands from admirals to apprentices, the following lessons focus on the emotional tone needed to get any enterprise started on the right foot. Think of it this way: The most brilliant strategies are useless piles of paper without superb people to carry them out. Recruiting the best people—from what, thanks to globalization, is now a worldwide pool of talent—comes first and long before Day One. Here's the leader's challenge: What welcoming tone will lure talented people who not only love the work the organization does but who will also mesh as a unified family? Where can we find and hire them before we even begin to build a roof over their heads?

Consider some answers.

WELCOME PEOPLE ABOARD BEFORE THEY'RE ABOARD.

Let's begin at the beginning. Whether you're sizing up a college campus, thinking of joining a civic group, or showing up on a new job, first impressions set the tone for all that follows. If you get a sense of order, discipline, and attention to detail, you know what to expect and what will be expected of you. Any hint of carelessness, shabbiness, or goofing off is a telltale that this is not a serious place. That's why it's crucial for any leader to make sure a newcomer to the enterprise gets off on the right foot.

As the captain of *Benfold*, I was determined that new shipmates would never get the kind of non-welcome I received on *Albert David*. When I was assigned new officers, I didn't wait for them to write; I sent them a welcome-aboard letter. That put the onus on them to respond to my letter—and it told me a lot about what kind of officer I was getting if I received a careless reply or none at all.

My letter told them what they could expect their jobs to be, and how they should begin to focus on and prepare for the assignment right away. I told them what our schedule was for the next few months, and sent a packet of information on San Diego, our home port, and its housing situation. I also sent a *Benfold* bumper sticker with the ship's motto, ONWARD WITH VALOR, and a *Benfold* baseball cap. It was a thick packet, and I meant it to be taken seriously. (An aside: We also created a similar program to welcome our new sailors.)

Once a newcomer comes aboard, it's a good idea to show a human side and a flash of humor during the orientation process. The late, great NFL coach Bill Walsh, who revolutionized professional football and led the San Francisco 49ers to three Super Bowl victories, was a master of this trick. In training camp, when the rookies were nervous about what to expect in their initial drug test, Walsh told them it was no big deal. "All they're going to do is ask for a little sample," he said—and he reached under his desk and pulled out a two-quart Mason jar. The room rocked with laughter, and the tension dissolved.

I'll be coming back to Bill Walsh often in the chapters that follow. Often called a genius for his cerebral approach to football, he was a model leader in his willingness to question authority, to challenge received wisdom, and to figure out new ways to capitalize on another team's shortcomings. His book *Finding the Winning Edge* has been called required reading for every coach—and other leaders can find lessons in it, too.

MAKE NEWCOMERS FEEL LIKE WINNERS.

When I came to *Benfold*, the program for welcoming new shipmates consisted of the same old tired procedure that had been used since time out of mind. Sailors would land at the airport and have to figure out for themselves how to get to the ship. Most were young and many came from rural areas. (If you drew a smile across the map of the United States, starting in Baltimore, Maryland, curving through the South and the heartland, and ending in Los Angeles, you would have a good idea of where most new recruits come from nowadays.) Their arrival experience was discouraging at best. They were nervous and scared to begin with, and when they finally got to the ship, no one seemed to know they were coming or had any process for getting them settled.

Soon after I arrived, the depth of dysfunction in this muddle was underscored when a young sailor got beaten up and robbed by a gang after he exited the base through the wrong gate on his first night aboard ship. He didn't know any better because no one had told him which gates to use. So I hauled in *Benfold*'s executive officer and our command master chief and told them that we owed our people better than this. I asked the executive officer (XO, in Navy lingo), who had a five-year-old daughter, to picture the girl joining the Navy after she turned eighteen. Then I told the two of them to work together to design a program to bring her aboard. They came up with such a great program that our squadron commander made a film of it as a model for welcoming newly reporting personnel.

I once gave a seminar at one of the regional Federal Reserve banks. Afterward, a senior vice president came up to me and said, "I get it now. I have a woman who works for me, and I have never been able to connect with her. It has been frustrating for both of us, and I have treated her horribly. As I sat there listening to you, it dawned on me that I should treat her the way I'd want my wife treated at work." Bingo! Treat your people and your shipmates the way you would want your spouse or child treated in the workplace.

On *Benfold*, new sailors were met at the airport and brought onboard to their quarters and their already-made beds. They met the command duty officer before being ushered into my cabin, from which they called their parents or spouse to report having made it safely to the ship. On the newcomers' first weekend, we showed them the base, the gym, the health club, and the commissary. We also took them off base to Sea World or the Hotel Del Coronado. We wanted them to feel right at home, not like strangers on a bad trip.

GIVE NEW RECRUITS A
PASSPORT TO SUCCESS.

To get its employees off on the right foot, Able Distributors, a Chicago-based wholesaler of heating and cooling equipment and products, sends new hires on the "Able World Tour." Whether a driver, warehouse person, secretary, or salesperson, a new hand's first assignment is to accompany a seasoned employee on a visit to the company's central distribution warehouse and three other sites where contractors come to place and pick up orders.

The new man or woman is introduced to every other person in the company, about fifty people. Besides creating a sense of immediate camaraderie, Michael Bleier, the founder's son and Able's vice president, uses the tour to introduce new employees to the company's most valuable—and valued—bit of cultural wisdom, which he describes this way: "The better we treat each other, the better we treat our customers."

The welcoming tour is followed by another piece of Michael's cultural indoctrination process. He hands each newcomer an "Able passport," which includes a list of to-do training and customer-service classes. For instance, rather than assume that a new employee knows the proper way to answer the phone or read back customer orders, Michael teaches a class on customer service and makes class attendance a passport requirement. Every new hire has to be checked off on these assignments within the first month of employment. The passport procedure itself adds a bit of fun to the training requirements and gives the company insight into a new hire's ability to complete assigned tasks in an efficient and timely fashion.

A GREAT CREW IS WHERE YOU
STRIVE TO FIND IT.

As a military commander, I had no voice in deciding who would be assigned to my ship. It was sheer luck that good people showed up. It was also my core challenge to make the best out of the hands we were dealt. I couldn't choose my crew.

But I could choose to help make them stronger. I'm proud to say that helping those folks become their best became a *Benfold* specialty. There's no point fuming about human resources. Work very hard with what you have and stand by for surprises, often happy ones. Of course, if you have a real choice in hiring, you can recruit people best suited for the job—and you'd be a fool to pass up the chance.

Civilian companies are limited in hiring only by their own imaginations. I particularly envy the managers of major sports teams who are both free and forced to create the most potent cocktails of brains and brawn imaginable. Jimmy Johnson, former coach of the Dallas Cowboys, once said that forming a pro football team essentially required "a chemist."

Surely it takes an emotional mixologist to concoct just the right brew of daring leaders, implacable followers, and human icebergs immune to blood and blame. But according to Tommy Lasorda, the longtime Dodgers manager, the baseball mix requires a talent scout even more than it does a chemist. His recipe calls for hunting and hiring two or three dominant stars as role models and clubhouse leaders. In turn, they help the manager control the team's two dozen other players, nearly all of them smoldering egotists—a trait that made them major leaguers in the first place.

A business needn't be glamorous to attract the right kind of help. Beating its rivals to the punch is all it needs. Consider the advantage seized by The Container Store, a nationwide chain of forty-two retail outlets selling ingenious storage gizmos. It dawned on the chain's leaders that its customers would make excellent employees. Accordingly, all staffers are asked to watch for likely prospects and are given a bonus of $500 for each customer hired as a full-timer and $200 for each one hired as a part-timer. The process includes ten-person interviews encouraging job candidates to show their personalities by offering sales ideas in a friendly group setting.

The Container Store now hires nearly a third of its workers from its customer base. Result: a turnover rate of less than 10 percent, compared with 70 percent for the company's competitors. The Container Store often goes as long as eight months without placing a single help-wanted advertisement.

It's also possible to spot candidates with a scarce trait—passion—and help them treat their jobs as more fun than work. Vail Horton is cofounder and chief executive officer of Keen Mobility, an Oregon-based maker of medical devices that improve the lives of the elderly and disabled. Himself born without legs or a fully developed right hand, Horton struggled tenaciously to overcome his handicaps and, while a student at the University of Portland, invented a crutch with a shock absorber to ease the chronic pain in his shoulders that ordinary crutches helped cause. He and his roommate, seeing the potential market for such devices, founded the business to help others overcome disabilities.

Now, when adding to his staff of seventeen, Horton screens potential recruits for their idealism, choosing candidates who care more about helping people than getting wealthy. He stresses that, in his company's open culture, anyone on the staff can come up with a new product, make it, and sell it. As a result, he says, Keen Mobility's workers have "enough passion to sustain them through a job that's extremely difficult."

At another small Oregon company, Tec Laboratories Inc., founder and CEO Steve Smith wants his thirty employees to have fun. He succeeds so well that, not long ago, his little pharmaceutical company was number one for the second year in *The Scientist* magazine's list of great places to work, competing with organizations employing as many as 5,000 people. With characteristic irreverence, Tec says its market is "the itch niche"—its products prevent and treat poison ivy, poison oak, and poison sumac, and repel outdoor insects and kill lice. Its prime customers include utility linemen, foresters, and firefighters.

The centerpiece of Tec's hiring process is a "foolproof interview," which consists of hours of meetings with managers, followed by more hours of meetings with prospective team members. It takes several days. "When the team finally buys into hiring somebody, they really like them," Smith told me, "so they're going to make that person successful."

Perhaps surprisingly for a company that prizes fun, a key issue for the interviewers is not the candidate's sense of humor but whether he or she can prove serious devotion to a cause. It might be any cause—Little League, Cub Scouts, a church or civic endeavor—as long as it involves active participation. People who do nothing other than work and watch television need not apply. Someone might have all the technical skills and a great-looking résumé, Steve explained, "but if they don't know what it feels like to be committed to something, we don't hire them." The fun at Tec Labs, it turns out, is a by-product of dedication to a mission well done. That was the case on *Benfold*, too, and I believe it's true in almost all really good organizations.

GET HIRING ADVICE FROM PEOPLE WHO REALLY UNDERSTAND YOUR NEEDS.

Never delegate hiring to those managers who may see job candidates less in terms of your needs than of their own egos. The danger is what Netscape cofounder Marc Andreessen calls "the law of crappy people. 'A' people hire 'A' people, but 'B' people hire 'C' people. The minute you let a weak manager in the door, they will hire individuals working for them who are even weaker. . . . Before you know it, your company degenerates."

According to Lawrence A. Bossidy, former CEO of AlliedSignal, the best way to check on candidates' performances is to ask their customers first and their supervisors only later.

Jeff Bezos, founder and CEO of Amazon.com, says that his employees have already been so conditioned to identify with customers that his company relies on employee judgments. "During our hiring meetings," he once wrote in the company's annual report, "we ask people to consider three questions before making a decision:

"1. Do you admire this person? For myself, I've always tried hard to work only with people I admire, and I encourage folks here to be just as demanding. Life is definitely too short to do otherwise.

"2. Will this person raise the average level of effectiveness of the group they're entering? We want to fight entropy. The bar has to continuously go up. I ask people to visualize the company five years from now. At that point, each of us should look around and say, 'The standards are so high now—boy, I'm glad I got in when I did!'

"3. Along what dimension might this person be a superstar? Many people have unique skills, interests, and perspectives that enrich the work environment for all of us. It's often something that's not even related to their jobs. One person here is a National Spelling Bee champion. I suspect it doesn't help her in her everyday work, but it does make working here more fun if you can occasionally snag her in the hall with a quick challenge: 'onomatopoeia!'"

HAIL TO (AND LEARN FROM) THE CHIEF.

Sooner or later, a new hire has to do the work expected and fit in. It can be the moment of truth when a job turns out to be different than expected. John Wade, one of my best young officers on *Benfold*, discovered this back in 1991, when he reported to his first ship, the destroyer *Arthur W. Radford*.

John was from an old Navy family—his grandfather, his father, and two uncles had all served—and he was well aware that Annapolis hadn't taught him everything he needed to know. So it was with more than a little humility that he approached the *Radford* chief petty officer in charge of the thirty-five operations specialists (radar operators) that John was nominally leading.

John's relatives, both officers and enlisted men, had often warned him about smart-alecky young officers who thought they knew everything when they first reported to ship. John cringed at ever being seen as such. So he told the chief he wanted to learn from him: "If he could help grow me, I promised, then I would be his biggest advocate. I would work my ass off for this division and this team."

John met the chief clutching his rookie ensign's binder of official training materials—presumably everything he needed to know to master his new job. The grizzled old chief took the binder from him and set it on a desk. "Mr. Wade," he said, "you'll get to this volume in due time. But right now, in order to lead the division effectively, you need to know this." He tossed a different book to John, and Wade caught it. It was the training requirements for the sailors he would be leading.

John practically inhaled that book, spent weeks standing watches with his sailors, and wound up knowing how to man the radar and performing their duties as well as they could. John was rightly proud of his achievement. He not only learned every job in his division, but also earned his sailors' respect as a good man and a good leader. You can't ask more of a junior officer.

John Wade, of course, credited his CPO for showing him the way. I could cite scores of similar cases. Chief petty officers are the backbone of the Navy and can be, in some ways, more useful than admirals. Successful officers in the Navy will tell you that they learned the most from their very first chief. As a beneficiary of their wisdom, I've been delighted to find CPO counterparts in business, too. They are the go-to people, the committed men and women who embody the corporate memory because they stay in their jobs while others come and go. They can make all the difference in how fast and how well a management trainee understands the business. Bottom line? Make sure your company teams up promising newcomers with your own chief petty officers.

Unfortunately, on most ships new sailors start off being matched with their division's poorest performer, mainly because poor performers have extra time on their hands. On *Benfold*, I wanted my new people to learn from the best, not the worst. In our welcome-aboard program, newcomers were matched with the number one sailor in their division. Sure, it was an extra burden for that great sailor, but with ability comes responsibility, and I wanted my new sailors to learn from the best. Who are your newbies learning from?

KEEP RECRUITING PEOPLE—EVEN AFTER THEY'RE ONBOARD.

I learned much of what I know about hiring (and leadership, for that matter) from President Bill Clinton's defense secretary Dr. William Perry. The secretary picked me, a decided dark horse, to be his military assistant in 1994. At the time, I thought he alone had made the decision, probably with the blessing of the senior military assistant, a two-star Army general named Paul Kern. A year later, I heard the real story from Dr. Perry himself.

While we were off on a trip together, I asked why he had hired me. "I didn't hire you," he said. "The staff did. I've been in business and government for forty years, and I know how to hire the smartest person. But that's never been a marker for my success." The real key, he said, was creating a team of people who would support one another to help him get the mission accomplished. "Out of the twelve candidates for the job, you were the only one who took the time to talk to the rest of the staff as if they were people," he said. "When I asked them who they wanted to work with, they said they wanted to work with you."

As you think about your own journey, ask yourself if you're the one with whom your fellow workers would choose to work. If not, is that important to you? It's something to think about.

After leaving the Navy, I found that a surprising number of senior managers don't know anything about their company's welcome-aboard program. They don't know how daunting it can be for new people to go through all the wickets with the human relations people, enrolling in the health-care plan, settling in at a desk, getting comfortable with their assigned computers, and getting access to the Internet—not to mention meeting their supervisors and colleagues. A more creative process would help new people start off on a much happier and less stressful note.

My chief engineer once told me that we were recruiting our people every day, even though we already had them aboard. Thinking of hiring as being a continuous process is a great incentive to keep people happy and productive—in short, to keep them. I work with companies that spend a lot of money recruiting the most promising candidates on college campuses. But that's where the recruiting process ends—a neglect that likely costs a lot more money and time than keeping workers happy and productive. If a company loses a promising trainee and has to recruit a replacement, it will spend at least twice as much to fill the position and waste a year of training in the process. If you're the manager in charge, you have the headache of repeating the training.

It's clearly in your own best interest to recruit your people every day, starting with Day One and never stopping. Make sure your recruits get off on the right foot, fired with enthusiasm and with the proper road map in hand. But the work doesn't stop there. A beginning is only a beginning, and the next step is to inspire all your people to hit the highest level they can possibly reach. That's the message of the next chapter.

CHAPTER 2

BUOY UP YOUR PEOPLE

INSPIRING EVERYONE TO BE THEIR BEST

To make any enterprise a winner, you have to persuade everyone involved in it to work at full intensity—to be the very best they can possibly be. But many younger people don't even know what excellence is, let alone what it looks, feels, and smells like. It's not that they are bad people, just that they have never had a role model to inspire them. Or maybe their friends always sneer at high achievers so they've settled for doing nothing but the minimum and just getting by. The challenge is to show these people excellence in action and then to inspire them to want it in their own lives, to make them take ownership of their jobs, and to demonstrate how they will benefit if the organization is a success. Excellence is not an abstract slogan. A great leader defines excellence and then inspires his team to exceed it by encouraging creativity and innovative business practices. It isn't easy, but it can be done.

Benfold's record is the proof. My crew was a random sample of Navy personnel—good, solid, hardworking sailors. But none of them had started life on the top rungs of the economic ladder. Many of the enlisted men and women had only high school educations. Some had been in trouble. Most of them saw the Navy as a stepping-stone to a good civilian job and were just putting in their time.

At first glance, this crew was not promising material. But as we all know—or should know—first glances can be deceiving, especially when it comes to judging human potential.

It's all about empowering all hands within limits, instilling confidence by constant training and drilling, showing respect for all jobs (including sewer control), creating crew-wide trust, giving people a personal stake in the ship's success, teaching everyone to learn from failure, and sailing ahead at flank speed through it all.

As Thomas A. Stewart, now the editor in chief of the *Harvard Business Review*, once suggested in *Fortune* magazine, an organization needs not only a mission statement but a *permission statement*—an understanding, written or tacit, that its people have the right to think, to respond to complaints, to disagree, and to make decisions within the guidelines set by the leader. At The Container Store branches, any sales clerk or cashier is allowed to take action to solve a customer's problem. If they make mistakes, the errors are probably no worse than the ones their managers would make. When General Electric analyzed a random sampling of its major mistakes, it discovered that none of them would have been prevented by one more stamp of executive approval.

In business as in the Navy, there are dozens of finicky rules that prevent people from taking the initiative and doing the right thing. When Gordon Bethune (who, incidentally, was a master chief petty officer in the Navy Reserve) and Greg Brenneman took over Continental Airlines as CEO and president, respectively, they inherited a nine-inch-thick book of just such rules, known around the airline as the "Thou Shalt Not" book.

Confronted with a mind-boggling labyrinth of dos and don'ts, most Continental employees did nothing they weren't explicitly told to do. Bethune and Brenneman signaled the dawning of a new day by taking a copy of the book out to the parking lot, dropping it into a steel drum, sloshing gasoline on it, and flipping in a lit match.

I tried to do the same for my crew. I couldn't burn the Navy's rule book, of course, but within the bounds of prudence, I could and did challenge some outdated regulations, bend others, and apply still others creatively to inspire my sailors to be their best. What my crew taught me in return was both humbling and exhilarating. I never imagined how often their responses would far exceed my hopes for them. Together, we came up with the following techniques for discovering the best in one another.

TAKE THE HELM, BUT STAY IN THE CHANNEL.

A Navy commander has access to very few of the motivational tools a corporate CEO can bring to bear. On top of that, we have to cope with the military's notoriously demotivating bureaucracy and hierarchy. I couldn't raise my sailors' pay or give them bonuses, and promotions were limited by the available Navy-wide vacancies and had to be earned through standardized advancement exams. But I could show my crew that their jobs were meaningful and important, and that everyone onboard would be a winner if *Benfold* became a top ship.

Empowerment, once the overused catchword in management seminars, has gained a bad reputation in business today, and I think the reason is because people don't really understand what empowerment signifies. To be empowered means you have an operating area, and you have the skills to make decisions in that area. But empowerment works only if those given power understand their limits and never cross them.

As leaders, we have to set limits for our people. They need to know that they can operate as they see fit within their channel but are not authorized to leave that channel. The leader needs to highlight the line that the empowered employee must not cross.

When a ship is at sea, Navy captains train a bright light on the do-not-cross line by supplementing so-called standing orders with night orders. Standing orders tell watch standers on the bridge, in the combat information center, and in the engineering plant what they are authorized to do and when they can do it. And if they need to take steps not specifically spelled out by their captain, the standing orders define the outside parameters of acceptable action. Every watch stander has to read the captain's standing orders at least once every three months to make sure he or she understands and can comply with the instructions.

But that's not all. Before turning in each night, the captain issues another set of orders, which tweak the standing instructions to take account of variables the crew might encounter such as the weather, the course of other ships in the area, equipment malfunctions or personnel changes, or any other issue that may have arisen since the standing orders were issued. The night orders set the boundaries for dealing with these anomalies. The sailors are empowered to steer the ship, but they must keep to a specified route.

TRAIN PEOPLE TO GO FULL SPEED AHEAD.

"Failing to prepare is preparing to fail," John Wooden, the fabled basketball coach, liked to say. My whole Navy experience repeatedly proved this maxim and its corollary: The harder you train, the bigger your triumph.

When Robert Stover arrived on *Benfold* as a junior lieutenant, for example, he didn't seem very promising. A slow-drawling ole boy from Arkansas, he had served on a poky amphibious ship with a top speed of twelve knots. Our high-tech destroyer was a different universe. Full speed ahead now meant thirty-one knots, with stuff coming at him fast, and he had never before had to make so many decisions so rapidly.

Even worse, the job I needed him to fill was anti-air warfare coordinator, perhaps the fastest and most complex job on the ship. In all honesty, I couldn't have done it myself. I didn't have the coordination. The job is best suited to a member of the Nintendo generation, with the concentration and coordinated reflexes to control dozens of planes in aerial combat and keep track of enemy positions, using both hands to punch all the buttons on a computer console and one foot to switch among several microphones. And even if your F-18s shoot down all the enemy planes, you've lost the battle if you don't have an aerial tanker in position with enough fuel to get the fighters back to the carrier. It is one of the most demanding jobs I know.

It took us four months to get Robert up to speed on that job. We focused our training on him. For much of that time, we were doing group training, exercising the whole fleet every day. We simulated air combat with our computerized internal systems, and Robert learned to deal with the computer, talk on the radio, keep a three-dimensional battle in his head, vector all the aircraft nearby, and remember each plane's fuel-consumption rate. By the end of the four months, he was a phenomenon.

He was so good that when the operations department head, Dave Hallisey, went off to a fellowship program, we fleeted Robert up to be his temporary replacement until the new department head came aboard. He had the desire and the ability, and we gave him the opportunity. And again, he measured up to and even surpassed expectations.

Training and staff development are never-ending tasks that require time, dedication, and investment, but they pay big dividends. Milliken, the textile manufacturer, requires workers to spend one week a year in training. General Electric and Motorola built their famously deep management teams through costly staff-development programs. And new employees at The Container Store average 241 hours of training—more than six full weeks—stretched out over their first year. It seems to work: The Container Store averages sales of $400 per square foot, versus just $125 for the rest of the housewares industry. And for eight straight years, the company has topped the *Fortune* list of the 100 best companies to work for.

James J. "Jamie" Maguire Jr. is a trainer and trainee extraordinaire. Maguire, CEO of the billion-dollar Philadelphia Insurance Companies, is a triathlete who has competed in two Ironman World Championship races on Hawaii's Big Island, which means he swims 2.4 miles in Kailua-Kona Bay, then jumps on his bike to pedal 112 miles across an expanse of lava rock before finishing up with a 26.2-mile run along the coast. "Grueling" hardly describes this kind of competition. But Maguire thrives on competition in business as well as sports, and he knows that training and preparation are essential to success in both.

To seize opportunities in specialty insurance, Maguire stresses thorough research by a committee of employees representing different areas of the company. Their diversity helps expose him to a variety of opinions. The best perspective, he explains, is usually the one you haven't heard yet.

To make sure his people get all the information needed to make good decisions, he has moved his company to an online client data system that covers businesses coast-to-coast. The system expands as his company grows, he says, thus benchmarking performance and backing up a leader who stresses continuous improvement. Although technology is critical to improving, having crew members who are intellectually in shape and inquisitive is even more critical.

Training pays off for employees at any company, especially in a time when advancing technology makes skills obsolete faster than ever before. If keeping up was ever optional, it's now mandatory. That point is underscored by Michael J. Critelli, CEO of Pitney Bowes, which used to be a maker of postage meters but has become a diversified technology center.

Critelli says he learned about dealing with change from his father, a printer with the Gannett Company in Rochester, New York. "When he started in training and development in 1963, there were 800 printers," Critelli told a Wharton audience. "When he retired in 1977, there were 260, and when he last returned for a visit in 1994, there were 14." Times are changing, and fast. We either manage that change on terms that are favorable to us or we become irrelevant.

GIVE YOUR PEOPLE ROOTS AND WINGS TO TURN THEM INTO LEADERSHIP MACHINES.

Roots and wings are what parents are often told to give their children: roots meaning solid skills and values, wings denoting the aspiration and confidence to go for the prize. No one is better at doing both for his business protégés than Norman Brinker, the restaurateur who founded Steak and Ale, then bought Chili's and built it into $1.2 billion Brinker International, a global chain of franchised family restaurants—750 of them, in locations from Seattle to Albania.

The list of Norman Brinker's protégés is a who's who of the food-service industry. They include Dick Rivera, a restaurant developer who heads Rubicon Enterprises; Rick Federico, CEO of P.F. Chang's; Lou Neeb, chairman of Mexican Restaurants; and Richard Frank, chairman and CEO of CEC Entertainment, the parent of Chuck E. Cheese's. All agree that Brinker has a remarkable gift for spotting good people, allowing them to learn from mistakes and firmly nudging them to reach for the stars. He gives people autonomy, unwavering trust, and opportunities to build self-confidence. After such mentoring, his alumni clearly have the wings to fly fast and high.

Equally important is Brinker's personal integrity. He banned shortcuts in dealing with customers, suppliers, and employees.

He insisted on fair treatment for all and instilled his core values in everyone who worked for him. In short, he gave them roots.

Long after moving to other jobs, Brinker's graduates stay in touch with him and he with them. He doesn't hesitate to pick up the phone and offer support. Like a good parent, he never stops encouraging those he cares about—an extended family almost too big to count.

Major companies with much greater name recognition have, in recent years, embraced a philosophy similar to Norman Brinker's. The big names realize that superb leadership is so rare that any company capable of growing it from the inside is miles ahead of its less nurturing competitors.

Such companies include General Electric, Goldman Sachs, Procter & Gamble, and Unilever. Their executive training programs and cultures are the envy of whole industries, their ideas as valued as hot stock tips. Goldman Sachs, for instance, not only outperforms its investment-banking peers, it also wields enormous influence well beyond the confines of the New York City financial district. A list of its alumni and their accomplishments tells the tale. Among the firm's former top people, Henry Paulson runs the U.S. Treasury Department, Robert Rubin chairs Citigroup, Jon Corzine governs New Jersey, Robert Zoellick heads up the World Bank, and Joshua Bolten is President George W. Bush's chief of staff. Goldman recruits the best, trains the best, and empowers its stars to deliver great results. While other major Wall Street institutions were getting mired in the subprime mortgage mess and writing off tens of billions in losses, Goldman shunned these risks and actually raised its earnings.

What are the golden precepts that put these giants on top? Joint research by consulting groups Hewitt and RBL Group has uncovered a set of best practices they think will work for just about any company. They advise us to:

• Invest time—yours plus your CEO's—and money; you can't develop leaders on a shoestring. GE's Jeffrey Immelt personally reviews the progress of the company's top 600 managers; Bill Hawkins of Medtronic devotes half his time to developing talent. While I was *Benfold*'s captain, I personally attended and participated in every major team training event.

• Pick out promising people early. Top companies begin developing leaders from the get-go, often spying good qualities in summer interns who are then offered permanent positions.

• Assign career-building jobs to help round out potential leaders and fill their experience gaps, as I did with Robert Stover. The hardest jobs tend to be most helpful in developing leaders; that's how they learn.

• Whenever possible, develop leaders within their current jobs. Rotating managers through assorted jobs is hard on company units and divisions. One way to fill any gaps in experience is to add short-term work assignments outside a person's area of expertise.

The military is becoming quite sophisticated in grooming future leaders. In the Air Force the high-potential candidates are groomed not just for their next job but for four or five jobs down the road. To prepare them to advance to each rung of their envisioned career ladders, the Air Force leaders figure out what skills each officer will need and then puts her or him in the jobs needed to develop those skills. If the perfect job doesn't exist at the right time, I'm told the higher-ups will actually create a job that incorporates the skills and responsibilities needed to train a promising candidate for a future leadership position.

• Give candid feedback and support. People can't learn unless they know what they're doing wrong—and right. Combine frequent assessments with help in overcoming failings. All successful leaders credit the mentoring they received along the way as critical to their success.

• Develop teams first. Training that is individually based can often be counterproductive, because the trainee frequently needs to see how her actions affect the entire team's productivity—say, salespeople, suppliers, or the IT department.

On *Benfold*, we always trained the team first. And once the team training was completed, we looked for any weaknesses that required remedial training to bring all individuals up to speed. That's not to say that team training covered everyone's needs. Individual sailors still required certain sets of skills regardless of whether they were on a team or not. By the same token, some skill sets were useless outside of the team environment.

Before the training started, everyone got together to talk about what the objectives were and how each individual's performance would contribute to the success of the overall goal. Then, at the end of the training session, everybody involved gathered to critique the training, reviewing the objectives and discussing each item line by line to assess whether all had been met. The team also looked at whether each individual had fulfilled his or her own specific goals. If the critique turned up a weak link among the team members, that's when an individual would be singled out for intense remedial training to assure everyone's full participation at the team level.

• Lead by inspiration rather than brute force. Although you may occasionally have to let people go, firing or demoting them routinely is counterproductive. Chances are, you'll lose knowledge, skills, and relationships you didn't even know you had because they are hidden somewhere within your knowledge-based environment. Better to work to win your crew's respect by giving them a sense of mission; they will be much more likely to do as you wish without pushback.

Back in the mid-1980s, when I was an aide to Admiral Hugh Webster in the Philippines, the life expectancy of an admiral's aide was very short. The admiral gets to pick whomever he wants, since it's a job that demands an exceptionally close relationship between the boss and his aide. An admiral's aide serves as the boss's right hand. The aide sits in on all the admiral's meetings, drafts all his correspondence, writes all his directives to the rest of the staff, and plans all his travel. You even play golf with the admiral if he wants to play golf. In fact, most admirals spend more time with their aides than they do with their spouses.

But even though the admiral makes his own selection, firings are still frequent. In the eighteen months I was in the western Pacific, 40 percent of the admirals' aides got fired because of incompatibility with either the boss or his spouse. But the turmoil in the western Pacific was nothing compared to the upheavals on another admiral's staff on the East Coast. The guy was merciless because he fired so many people, from commanding officers to staff personnel. But this admiral was particularly hard on his aides. Every one of them was apparently lacking. No matter that

he interviewed every candidate himself and made all his own se-
lections, he still lopped off a record number of heads.

On one occasion, the admiral instructed the Bureau of Naval
Personnel to send him an unmarried man. The bureau duly responded, nominating a man whose records showed him to be single. The admiral interviewed the fellow, never asking him about
his personal life, and the officer didn't think, or didn't choose, to
mention that he was engaged to be married. He got the job, and
between the time he detached from his previous ship and the time
he reported for duty with the admiral, he also got married and his
wife left her own job to join him in his new home port. Then,
when the new flag lieutenant showed up and announced himself
a married man, the admiral fired him on the spot!

Brute force, though, typically has unexpected consequences, as
this admiral soon learned. Refusing to allow him to ruin any more
officers' careers, the Bureau of Naval Personnel declined to send
him even one more sacrificial lamb. The admiral's bad behavior
had finally caught up with him, and he would no longer be allowed to run roughshod over the bureau personnel or his poor
subordinates.

• Embed leadership development in your culture. Turning
people into leaders isn't the flavor of the week or month; it should
be part of the way the organization lives day to day. Mentoring,
feedback, and civic involvement must be the accepted norm, not
procedures that are merely being tolerated for the short term.

If your crew hasn't already demanded that you put more focus
on developing leaders, it soon will. Young people understand
how the economy is changing even if you don't, and they want
to be prepared to succeed. By the same token, a reputation for

developing talent is a selling point for companies trying to attract top recruits. And once that reputation is established, it creates a virtuous circle: As your company steps up its performance, it attracts ever more talented people who join your crew and keep the ship sailing at flank speed.

The leadership at Goldman Sachs has long enjoyed a golden reputation on Wall Street, and the performance of the firm's top people during the 2007 subprime mortgage debacle has only polished their standing. What struck me in an article that appeared in the *Wall Street Journal* on November 1, 2007, as the bad news continued to unfold was the stark contrast between the crisis response of Goldman CEO Lloyd Blankfein and that of James Cayne at Bear Stearns.

During a particularly critical stretch in mid-July, when two big Bear Stearns hedge funds were going belly up and writing off $1.2 billion of investors' money, Cayne spent ten days at a Nashville, Tennessee, bridge tournament—without a cell phone or immediate access to e-mail. Nor did Cayne vary his summertime golf ritual, leaving work early on Thursday afternoons to spend a good chunk of that day and the next three on the golf course, apparently unconcerned that his club's rules left him virtually incommunicado at a critical time for his business. Having a great team in place and trusting them is important, but in a time of crisis, a great captain is always on deck.

In contrast, Blankfein chose to remain on deck to steer his ship through a crisis. He canceled his August vacation plans altogether, sacrificing the time he had planned to spend with his sons before they left for college to keep watch over the deteriorating mortgage situation. The Goldman chief reportedly made frequent visits to his firm's mortgage trading floor, not only to lend support to his people but also to make real-time decisions as needed.

When the news of Goldman's profit gains broke in November 2007, I wasn't surprised. Goldman Sachs, it turned out, had reduced its mortgage-related portfolio and protected itself against losses on its remaining risky mortgages, while the likes of Bear Stearns, Merrill Lynch, and Citigroup were barreling headlong into the abyss.

LET GREAT PLAYERS BE GREAT.

By definition, highly gifted people are different. Often they behave and perform in odd ways that upset bosses and others with rigid expectations. If this ever happens to you, congratulations— not every leader is lucky enough to employ oddballs with unique talents.

Take your cue from Johnny Bunn. While coaching basketball at Stanford University in the 1930s, Bunn was approached by a nervous freshman who asked if his peculiar goal-shooting style would keep him off the team.

The boy, Hank Luisetti, used only one hand; all the other players at that time used two hands for any shot attempt over five feet away. Bunn asked Hank to demonstrate. After watching him rapidly sink a barrage of long one-hand jumpers, the coach welcomed Hank aboard, realizing that he might well be creating basketball history. Indeed, he was: Hank Luisetti and his jumper went on to revolutionize the game, earning him a place in the Basketball Hall of Fame.

From my perspective, the big winner was Johnny Bunn, a

coach who spotted greatness in a form then considered eccentric and immediately refused to change it.

DIG DEEP AND PULL UP.

At Aflac, the giant insurer based in Columbus, Georgia, senior vice president and deputy chief administrative officer Teresa White thinks the role of a manager is "digging deep and pulling up." In the beginning of a new assignment, she told me, "You start by going deep," actually learning every aspect of the operation "to understand what your systems are doing, what your process is delivering, and what your people are delivering from that process. Once you understand that, you pull up," by turning over as much responsibility as possible to employees.

Teresa is frank about this pulling-up business. She goes to her charges and tells them, "I am pulling up, and that means these responsibilities won't be mine anymore. They'll be yours." She lists the jettisoned tasks in writing and asks those newly responsible to sign off, thus formalizing their assumption of the duties.

Some people are eager to sign, she has found, while others are apprehensive. But Teresa doesn't back off: "You've got to let them know you've been taking some of the weight off them just by being there and staying involved, but now you're pulling up." And there are no trial runs. Teresa won't backstop the newly empowered, not even for a week or two. Confident that she knows when it's time to pull up, she draws a clear line between what was once her responsibility and what is now someone else's. "It is important to make sure your team members are clear on their roles so they have a fair shot at being successful. As a leader, it is my responsibility to ensure that my team is well-informed." And if that isn't clear, what is?

SPEND TIME IN THE SEWAGE SYSTEM— EVEN THE GUY IN THE LOUSIEST JOB NEEDS TO KNOW HE'S VITAL.

"Don't make the mistake of thinking you can lead with your feet up on the desk," said Lawrence A. Bossidy, former head of Allied-Signal. "If you're responsible for sales and marketing, you should be in the field talking to customers, not just managing the sales force from your office. If you're the head of R&D, you should be visible in the lab to see what's happening. If you're in charge of human resources, you should be on the factory floor to determine what's on the minds of your employees."

I agree. Leading is largely people-watching, a constant process of seeing and being seen all over your enterprise. For me, that meant climbing all over *Benfold*, especially down the ladder to the ship's weakest link—its sewage system. All the waste wound up in the contaminated holding tank at the very bottom of the ship, and just one technician, Shaun Perkins, had the job of maintaining the pumps that kept the sewage flowing in and, ultimately, out. The problem was poorly engineered mechanical seals in the pumps, which kept Shaun constantly fighting leaks.

It was a crappy job in every sense, made even worse by the fact that, to get to the pump room, you had to inch your way down four sets of steel rungs set in a vertical tunnel about half the size of an elevator shaft. In heavy seas, it was a nightmare; sailors have fallen and seriously injured themselves going up and down those ladders.

Every other day, I made a point of visiting Shaun at his post. I couldn't do much about his conditions, but I could tell him that he was doing a great job, and we depended on him to keep the ship operating. It was a pain in the butt to climb down four flights to get to the literal bowels of the ship and then climb back up again. But the payoff was worth it. Shaun really did do a great job, and he wore his *Benfold* cap at an especially rakish tilt after my visits.

Shaun also stepped outside his rating and volunteered to be trained as a rescue swimmer. If a sailor fell overboard or if we were conducting a rescue at sea, Shaun would put on the scuba gear and go into action. Being a rescue swimmer is one of the most dangerous and grueling specialties in the Navy. It's hard to find volunteers and the dropout rate from the school is high, because the course in lifesaving techniques and rescue swimming is so physically demanding.

The pride and self-confidence that led Shaun to volunteer for such a brutal task weren't misplaced. When he took the SAT test offered onboard ship, he scored 1,290; many a graduate from even top high schools can only dream of such a score. He went on to earn a degree in civil engineering and did well at it until, tragically, he was killed in a motorcycle accident. That news hit me hard, because Shaun was such an outstanding young man.

His whole life underscored a critical lesson for me: If you make people feel they're crucial to the success of the operation, even if they're doing work that seems trivial or demeaning, they'll take great pride in it—and they'll be members of the go-to team, both for you and for themselves. Shaun was a charter member of my go-to team, and everyone who knew him misses him terribly.

The Shaun Perkinses of this world are the kind of people every organization should set out to identify and motivate if it hopes to add value to the bottom line.

MIND THE GAP.

When three bombs blasted through the London Underground during the morning rush hour on July 7, 2005, it was Britain's worst terrorist incident since the 1988 downing of Pan Am Flight 103 over Lockerbie, Scotland. Fifty-six people were killed and some 700 injured by the three suicide bombers below ground and a fourth on a city bus. It would take investigators days just to sort out what had happened. But for all the carnage, devastation, and confusion, nearly the whole Underground network was up and running in time for the next morning's rush.

That wasn't just luck. It came about because the Underground's front-line employees calmly and confidently stepped in and handled the crisis. "We evacuated 250,000 people out of our tunnels and trains during rush hour, and not a single person was injured," according to Tim O'Toole, the Underground's managing director and chief executive. "That doesn't happen because of management intervention. That happens because people in the field are in control and understand what needs to be done. The thing that makes 14,000 people behave that way is training and competence."

What O'Toole might have said is that he has been minding the gap at the London Underground. The phrase "mind the gap" refers to the danger of stepping into the void between the train and the platform at the Underground stations. O'Toole, who learned about trains while running the Conrail freight system in the

United States, has been laboring since 2003 to close the training, equipment, and performance gap so he can turn around the ancient, decaying Underground, known to Londoners as the Tube. Once world-renowned, the world's oldest subway is plagued by antiquated signals, crumbling stations, worn-out track, and cars as old as forty years. And all this must be fixed while the system carries 3.5 million passengers every day. "We've got to perform heart surgery on this patient while he plays tennis," O'Toole often jokes. The reforms had to cope with delays and cost overruns, but he is confident that the job will be finished by the time the 2012 Olympics are held in London.

When he took over, O'Toole found that his first problem was a hostile, demoralized workforce. As one worker challenged him, "With 60 million people on this island, what do we need you for?" They feared that his reforms would cost jobs and make their lives more difficult. He set out to cure that by increasing training, knowing that making workers more competent would help instill morale-boosting confidence and make them more cheerful and courteous to passengers.

Drilling and training are ongoing for Tube workers, and, well before the 2005 bombings, they had simulated crises including biological and chemical attacks—drills that clearly helped prepare them for the chaos of that day. O'Toole also pushes employees to get National Vocational Certification, known as NVQs, in their fields of training. "We want our people to understand that they know things that other people don't know," he explained. Today, the Tube has more NVQ holders than any other British company.

O'Toole hopes to bend the system's rigid seniority and work rules, training each employee to perform multiple jobs that would make their lives more interesting and rewarding. A worker might drive a train for two hours, for instance, and then spend another two hours interacting with passengers as a station agent. Whatever happens, O'Toole and his people can be confident that they're on top of their jobs. They already aced the test on July 7, 2005.

SET YOUR PEOPLE UP TO SUCCEED.

Just because you're a graduate of the Naval Academy and captain of a ship doesn't mean you necessarily have the right experience to handle every tricky situation. I showed up on *Benfold* without any real idea of how to keep racial tensions from bubbling over. What I did have was a negative example from my days on a previous ship, where an African-American crew member had been belittled by the captain, which only exacerbated whatever discord might have been brewing. I certainly didn't want to sail in that captain's wake.

Tony Arzu, my assistant operations officer, was also my senior-most African-American officer. Tony was smart and capable, but he, too, came to me from a slow ship that hadn't prepared him for the complexity of his assignment on *Benfold*. I wanted Tony to succeed, but, more important, I needed him to succeed; I wanted him to serve as a role model and mentor to the young African-American enlisted sailors on the ship.

Here was my dilemma: I don't believe in racial quotas, but I strongly believe that management ranks should roughly mirror the demographics of your crew. I learned that lesson from Don Loren, who captained a frigate when I was working at the Bureau of Naval Personnel assigning officers to ships. I dealt directly with commanding officers to find the best people for the jobs they needed to fill.

Don called me one day and said, "Mike, I need you to assign an African-American officer to my ship." In my two years on the job, I had never received such a request and I told him so. He explained that 15 percent of his workforce was African-American but he didn't have even one African-American officer in his officers' mess (called the wardroom). He said he wanted to have a role model in the wardroom so that his African-American sailors would have someone to turn to for mentoring, coaching, and guidance.

Don Loren later went on to be selected for admiral. Of all the captains I worked with at the time, he was among the more enlightened, and he taught me that giving any minority group someone to look up to is a good thing. The idea for making Tony Arzu a role model for the young African-American sailors on *Benfold* was a result of Don's influence.

But I also knew that if I left Tony to sink or swim in his tough new position he might founder—and that would be bad both for Tony and for those I hoped would look up to him. So I decided to ease him into his new role in ways that would allow him to build up victories, confidence, experience, and, most important, stature in the eyes of his shipmates—of all colors. He became a standout watch stander in our combat information center. The ultimate compliment for an officer is when a sailor says he or she can sleep well at night with you on watch, and the crew slept soundly when Tony Arzu was on watch.

The bottom line is that you can't tell your crew members whom to look up to, but you can put worthy people in positions where they can excel and earn their shipmates' respect and admiration.

With a little nudge from me, Tony Arzu got the chance to prove himself to his mates. And he did a phenomenal job.

HELP PEOPLE OVER THE HURDLES.

When you want people to be their best, you have to mean their all-around best—not just doing their job to the best of their ability. That means helping them straighten out their personal lives if need be and encouraging them to excel in activities outside of work.

In talking recently with Darren Barton, one of my Tomahawk mission planners on *Benfold*, I was reminded of what, in retrospect, sounded like almost nonstop self-improvement schemes dreamed up by the captain. As you might expect, in the military we are supposed to stay in good physical condition. In the Navy, we have to take a physical readiness test twice a year that includes a 1.5-mile run and sit-ups and push-ups in a certain time frame. It's important that leaders be physically fit if their people have to be.

So I created the Captain's Physical Fitness Challenge. Anyone who beat me in the run got a four-day weekend. Please note that the challenge applied only to the run and not the sit-ups. While I was blessed with long legs, I was never blessed with six-pack abs, so the Captain's Challenge was geared to my strength. I know it's not exactly fair, but we have an acronym in the Navy: RHIP. It stands for "rank has its privileges," and as one of the older crew members, I needed every advantage I could possibly get.

Darren Barton busted his butt to beat me, but he never could. Shaun Perkins routinely outran me without *ever* seeming to have broken a sweat. I have to admit that Darren remembers correctly when he says that some of the "crusty old chiefs" on *Benfold* also beat me. But that was half the fun for all of us.

Darren himself now deals with Navy personnel issues and getting the best job performance out of people, having earned a chief petty officer rating since our days together on *Benfold*. He told me of a situation where the mother of one of his sailors had to have surgery to remove a brain tumor. Darren saw to it that the young man got home to be with his mother, even though the ship was deployed at sea. As he says, whether it's a kid who's homesick, a wife with a family problem, a shipmate with a drinking issue, or any other kind of major distraction, the Navy wants to help its sailors.

For strictly business reasons you have to give your people the help they need, because when their minds are on their own problems they aren't doing engine maintenance properly or paying attention to the missile-launch sequence or seeing an incoming missile on the radar screen. In other words, they aren't doing their jobs, and that affects everyone, particularly so in a hothouse environment like that of a ship at sea. But you also lend a hand because it's the right thing to do.

Work hurdles can be addressed in various ways. The Navy's annual evaluations, in which people must be ranked against their colleagues, can make or break careers as well as create rivalry where there should be cooperation. So on *Benfold* I gave feedback on a quarterly basis to help my officers and chiefs correct problems before the crucial annual review. I was careful to explain clearly what the criteria would be for the best rankings. I never wanted someone to be surprised at his or her annual evaluation. If anyone was, then it was my fault for not setting the proper expectation.

I've also found that people often become their best selves—and solve some problems for you—when you give them responsibility. When I arrived on *Benfold*, I was burdened by an officer who apparently disliked one of the petty officers in her division, Matt Blackman, and often berated him in public.

Matt was extremely bitter. I discovered that he was doing the work of a first-class petty officer and doing it very well. One of his jobs was running the ship's store, which meant handling a lot of cash. Profits went to the crew's recreational fund. But there were no profits; the store had been stocked with stuff no one wanted to buy. So the recreational fund was empty.

In my opinion, the disbursing officer was abrasive to her people. She was soon transferred elsewhere, but not through any act of mine; her transfer had been in the works before I arrived. It was certainly welcomed by her subordinates. Nevertheless, it raised the issue of how some managers deal with problem employees— or, rather, how they *don't* deal with problem employees.

A manager who sloughs off such problems is being neither loyal nor helpful to the organization. Transferring your problems elsewhere is a cop-out, not a solution. From that experience, I vowed to solve our personnel problems and not transfer them elsewhere because it was the expedient thing to do.

George Lynett, our new supply officer, put Matt in charge of the store. Soon after, Matt designed and ordered cool-looking *Benfold* T-shirts that kept selling out. I wore one myself. These and other innovative items quickly gave *Benfold* one of the Navy's most profitable ship's stores, to say nothing of a booming recreational fund. Matt went on to be promoted again and also won a Navy Achievement Medal. Thanks to a little inspiration and the benefits of responsibility, one man's redemption became a whole crew's treasure.

CHANGE THE WAY THE CREW
LOOKS AT FAILURE.

Motivating people involves a constant process of teaching, which includes not just facts but values and attitudes. One of the great lessons that the late Bill Walsh taught his 49ers was that a failure is less important than what you do to correct it. Former offensive lineman Bruce Collie remembers getting a holding penalty that cost the team a touchdown. After the game, waiting for the inevitable film review on Monday, "I was sick about it," Collie said later. "I couldn't sleep." And in the films, at the end of that play, Walsh stopped the projector. Collie braced himself to get flayed. But Coach Walsh said, "We all know what Bruce did on that play, but I want you to see what he did on the next one."

On the next play, angry at himself for his mistake, Collie had driven a defensive lineman back and flattened him. Walsh showed it, stopped the projector again, and said, "This is what I want you to do after you make a mistake. You don't need to be thinking about your mistakes. Do something constructive about them." And Collie concluded, "That was Bill Walsh. He changed the way I looked at failure that day."

MAKE EMPLOYEES PROUD OF WHAT THEY DO.

People often speak disparagingly of burger flipping as a dead-end job; I've been guilty of it myself. But the best fast-food franchises know that the key to keeping customers happy is to make sure the staffers take pride in their jobs and understand why each is vital to the success of the business.

The best such operation I've seen is In-N-Out Burger, a West Coast chain. Their restaurants are meticulously clean, their burgers are fantastic, and each restaurant has a staffer who does nothing but cut the chain's homemade french fries. You can watch this employee in a picture window stuffing potatoes through the machine as you navigate the drive-through.

In-N-Out hires workers who are friends of people already on the payroll, on the theory that groups of friends will enjoy working together and stay on the job longer. The chain also provides health benefits—a rarity these days in much more prestigious jobs. As a result, In-N-Out Burger has one of the highest retention rates in the fast-food industry. It's not at all unusual for the chain's managers to have been in the business for thirty or forty years and to have moved up from flipping burgers. Every time you go to an In-N-Out store, you see young kids smiling and having a good time. They are motivated.

So motivated, in fact, that the service at In-N-Out goes beyond excellent. Not long ago, when I was in Sacramento, California, to give a speech, I was talking with my driver about the chain. He topped all of my stories by telling about being in an In-N-Out store where a man told the manager that the newspaper vending machine was out of *USA Today* and asked if any more copies were lying around. The manager said, "I'll take care of it." He walked out of the store, vaulted a brick wall, went to the 7-Eleven next door, and bought a copy of *USA Today*, which he handed to his customer. You tell me: Is that customer going to come back? I will never again denigrate burger flippers. Be the best at whatever you choose to do, and you will be respected.

PUT PEOPLE IN CHARGE OF
THEIR DESTINY, NOT THEIR WORK.

I thought I was showing my sailors how to be their best from Day One on *Benfold*, but, as it turned out, I was wrong. I tried to define what excellence is and why it is important, and to make the crew realize they were part of it. I explained that if we did the job right, the payoff would come in gaining control of our own schedule.

For instance, when we were in port, I'd tell my sailors that if they got all the maintenance chores done on Friday mornings, they could have Friday afternoons off to spend at home with their families or doing the personal chores and shopping that would otherwise eat into their weekends. Similarly, we might be able to reduce our time at sea. We were supposed to spend twenty-seven days at sea every three months, training in various exercises until we passed all the tests. I tried to get across to the crew that if we passed the tests more quickly, we might spend only twenty-four days at sea, or twenty-one, and have more time in port with our families.

But nothing I said ever really sank in until we aced the certification process. When a ship returns from a deployment and finishes routine maintenance, it has to be certified as ready for its next assignment—a program of training and assessment that the Navy can stretch out for six months. When *Benfold* returned from duty in the Persian Gulf in 1998, I said we were going to get certified in just one week, an immodest boast that drove some old Navy dinosaurs up the wall. But thanks to some new training methods and computer programs the crew had developed on their own, at the end of Week One, *Benfold* had achieved the highest readiness score ever.

Then I persuaded the admiral that he could save a lot of costly fuel by cutting our time at sea from six months to two months, and letting us go on port visits up and down the West Coast for a good part of those two months. My sailors were in hog heaven going ashore at Puerto Vallarta and Cabo San Lucas in Mexico, at San Francisco, and at Vancouver in Canada. They had earned it—and their reaction was, "Well, now I get it; now I understand what being in control of your own schedule means."

It was an epiphany for me, too. It suddenly hit me that they hadn't understood what they stood to gain. They were working hard only because I was ordering it and praising them for the results. In hindsight, my failure was talking about controlling our "schedule." For one thing, the word itself is a bureaucrat's term, and in no way inspiring. I didn't do a good enough job defining excellence. More important, controlling the schedule is just the beginning of the payoff anyone can reap from working up to his or her potential.

I don't know how many business meetings I've sat through where the CEO stands up and says, "We've got to increase business by 15 percent, year over year." Growing the bottom line by 15 percent is the new rallying cry, but when I look at the blank faces of the audience members, it's clear they are not inspired. Sure, they'll work to meet their quotas, but so what? The CEO hasn't thought to provide context, to let people know that 15 percent (or whatever the growth number happens to be) will show investors that the company has its act together and convince customers that the company will be in business next year and for many years to come.

A better way to describe the potential rewards of excellence is what I said in Chapter 1 and what I preach to my audiences: You can actually control your own destiny. Most people are at the mercy of events and other people's priorities. But if you work hard enough, do your absolute best, and take ownership of your job, you can take charge of what happens to you. You will have earned the right to call your own shots.

SPRINKLE A BIT OF SEASONING
OVER YOUR CREW.

My good friend Marc Jacobson, who runs his own financial services company, believes that training people properly is absolutely the best way to put them in charge of their own destiny and help them to become their best selves. And he does that not only by modeling the preferred behavior himself but by exposing his people to veterans who perform with excellence every day on the job.

Marc, who became associated with Prudential Insurance about six years ago, says that a lot of younger agents never have the chance to learn from the old hands. When you're just breaking into the business, you spend most of your time manning the phones and pounding the sidewalks to drum up business. There is some basic training, of course, but you never really get to see the top performers in action. You never see them demonstrate excellence. Marc designed what he calls "Top Gun" seminars to remedy that shortcoming by having seasoned personnel come in to teach newcomers about the art of selling life insurance and annuities.

I wasn't surprised when Marc told me that he initially had a hard time convincing Prudential managers to buy into his Top Gun concept. Many leaders resist empowering people for fear that they'll overstep their bounds and threaten the leader's authority. They just can't accept that it's "our" ship and that success depends on every person working to capacity. But Marc is no shrinking violet, and even though he was relatively new to Prudential, he went straight to the top to sell his idea to the president, John Greene. Insurance companies sometimes get bad raps from their customers. This masks the overwhelming numbers of insurance people I have met who, like Marc, are dedicated and motivated and try to do the right thing by their customers.

Impressed by Marc's conviction about the worth of his program and his willingness to stick his neck out by coming directly to the president, Greene signed on to the idea. Marc set up the first meeting and brought in the company's top performers to act as mentors for the inexperienced salespeople—giving them selling tips and encouraging them to keep rowing toward their goals.

After six months, the sales figures for those who attended the seminar were up by an average of 22 percent, while the newcomers who didn't take part saw their sales decline by an average of 7 percent. Marc was happy to be vindicated, but he was even happier to see the young guys succeed because of his efforts.

Sometime later, after Marc had opened his own shop, his efforts to empower crew members by modeling excellence paid off in a most gratifying way. He told me that one of his agents, without any direct prodding from him, took it upon herself to shepherd a client's claim all the way through the filing and payment process. Aware that the client was suffering from brain cancer, this agent simply wanted to make sure that the client didn't suffer any undue stress or aggravation in pursuing the insurance claim. When Marc asked her why she'd done it, she said, "I knew that that's what you'd want."

As Marc says proudly, behavior like that comes from the top down, from empowering and training. "But more important," he adds, "if you can show your employees that you care, they will take care of your clients." And how does Marc show that he cares? By treating people with respect, he says, which, for Marc, means asking his staff members how things are going, how their families are doing, and publicly praising good work. Too many business owners, he says, are so focused on their clients and the crush of day-to-day business that they overlook what's going on with their staff, to say nothing of the world outside their executive suites. All too many lack the generous spirit of Marc himself. Imagine their reaction when he recently won $30,000 in a charity raffle and immediately contributed it back to the sponsors.

When you listen to Marc describe how he molds and trains his crew, it sometimes sounds very simple. But, as he is fond of saying: "It's simple but it's not easy."

Inspiring people to be their best is a never-ending job that also brings out the best in a leader. You have to give yourself reminders and sometimes take extra pains to give your people chances to succeed, as I did when I arranged for the SAT test administrator to be flown to *Benfold* at sea. But a large part of the job is done almost by instinct, as naturally as breathing. And like most qualities of leadership, inspiring your people has a crucial requirement: that both you and they tell the truth, without sugarcoating or phony reassurances. That's the subject of the next chapter.

CHAPTER 3

NO MORE AYE-AYE MEN (OR WOMEN)

CULTIVATING TRUTH-TELLING

FOR NEARLY THREE CENTURIES NOW, EVER SINCE THE PHIlosophers of the Enlightenment taught humankind the value of rational thinking, it's been a truism that you can't make good decisions unless you know the facts. But it sometimes seems that half the judgments in the world are made in outright defiance of reality.

In some cases, bad decisions are the product of "experts" being too cocksure to wade through a jungle of footnotes to find the truth. Instead, they simply go along with the crowd. At other times, leaders are deceived about the true situation by people afraid to tell them the truth. From the charge of the Light Brigade to Custer's last stand, military history teems with cases of commanders receiving careless or misleading information, saluting smartly, and heading into a defeat that the truth could have prevented. But this age-old lesson never seems to sink in.

And with reason—bad reason. Throughout known history, messengers of bad news have flinched from delivering it to irascible or self-deluded rulers for fear of losing their lives or at least their jobs in the process. In his tragedy *Antigone*, for example, Sophocles depicts Creon, king of Thebes, becoming so enraged at a bad-news messenger that he kills him on the spot. The irony of this Persian Messenger Syndrome, as some call it, is the recipient's illusion that killing the messenger will kill the bad news. Instead, it often kills the recipient, who winds up destroyed by the facts he refused to hear.

Many say that President George W. Bush and his administration, having decided to invade Iraq and do it fast and on the cheap, listened only to those "facts" that would support their decisions. They also say that Defense Secretary Donald Rumsfeld made plain what he wanted to do, and Vice President Dick Cheney and his staff pressured the intelligence agencies to produce trumped-up reports that would justify the invasion.

We may never know what truly happened, and it may be that those at the top did not feel they were pressuring subordinates. However, it certainly gives the appearance that those at the top were surrounded by aye-aye men and women who were only too happy to say what they knew their bosses wanted to hear, and that the rosy scenario was the only plan discussed. The lonely few who tried to plan for other outcomes—as when Army General Eric Shinseki testified to Congress that the invasion would take many more men than Rumsfeld was sending—soon found themselves vilified and sidelined. Shinseki was even humiliated at his retirement ceremony, when no senior civilians showed up. To those in uniform, the pettiness was appalling.

Leaders who should be guarding against soothing lies instead send clear signals about what they want to hear, reward the aye-aye chorus that sings it, and punish anyone who tries to set them straight. They produce a climate in which even good people with distinguished careers are afraid to tell the truth and will do whatever it takes to give their bosses the answers they want. The situation in Iraq is only the latest proof that wishful thinking can be disastrous.

The Navy certainly isn't immune to the aye-aye malady. In my own time in the service, a talented commander—I'll call him John—won fame as a martyr to unguarded truth-telling. John was giving a briefing when an admiral made a comment that clearly showed that the admiral didn't know what he was talking about. John sensed that the misunderstanding could result in a disastrous order, so he said, very respectfully, "Admiral, that's not correct." The admiral was outraged at being contradicted in an open session and removed John's name from the list of officers to be given command of a ship. For the next two years, as long as the admiral was on active duty, John's advancement was in limbo. When the admiral retired, the Navy finally gave John a new command. But the lesson was plain to everyone: You tell the truth at your own peril.

If telling the truth can be judged a mistake, lying should be judged a mortal sin. But in the military, as in business, lies go unpunished far too often. They may simply be swallowed and ignored even though they are transparently untrue. The most outrageous case I've personally witnessed was on my first ship, the *Albert David*, off the coast of the Philippines. Our battle group was doing gunnery practice, shooting at a huge target made of concrete and steel that was kept afloat with pockets of air. Several ships had scored direct hits, but the target wouldn't sink. Near sunset, we had to do something to get rid of it; it was close to shipping lanes and we couldn't just leave it there.

The commodore, who was on our ship, ordered the captain to come alongside the target, put a boarding team on it, and set charges to blow it up. But the captain handled *Albert David* clumsily and ran right over the target, scraping the hull from stem to stern. The target damaged the underwater sonar dome and mangled three of the five blades of the ship's propeller. The propeller had to be replaced after we limped back to Subic Bay.

When the admiral demanded to know how all this had happened, the commodore and the captain seemed mystified. They said they first learned about the damage when a sonarman on one of the other ships heard our propeller clanking. I know this because Chief Dooley showed me their reporting on the incident. For all they knew, a sea monster had attacked *Albert David*—and done it so sneakily that no one had noticed anything.

The repairs cost millions of dollars and put the ship out of action for six weeks. Everyone onboard knew what had happened and when. The thump of the target as the ship passed over it was impossible to ignore. But when our captain heard that an officer had told one of his friends on the admiral's staff about it, he went ballistic.

With some of us junior officers watching, he threatened to punch the officer in the mouth. With fists clenched and veins bulging in his neck and forehead, the captain stopped himself from throwing the punch, but the message was clear: Don't tell the truth. And the message was reinforced when the admiral turned a blind eye to the whole fiasco.

There are other cases, less blatant, in which facts are covered up with no intent to do harm. Intended or not, however, damage can be done—and a leader must be constantly on guard not to be deceived by the aye-aye men.

Darren Barton's post-*Benfold* job is as an instructor at a training command, responsible for teaching aspiring captains, commodores, and admirals in the use of the Tomahawk missile. Darren knows full well the value of truth-telling, since mistakes could be costly if any of his "students" left school with bad information.

"As a leader, you don't know everything, you don't always have the best ideas," Darren rightly pointed out to me. "Sometimes your people have a better idea. And you need that pushback." But since all of his students outrank him, Darren's world is like a microcosm of the naval hierarchy—and of the business one, for that matter—where disagreement implies criticism, and is often met with stony silence or outright anger. Diplomacy, Darren maintains, is key.

In his chief petty officer's training role, Darren has to tell people when they're not doing their jobs correctly, but he couches his criticism in terms of helpfulness. "Here's how we are going to help you do better," he tells them. Of course, it's easier to be diplomatic when your goal is not to play "gotcha," but genuinely to help someone succeed. If you can help your boss avoid a mistake or if you can catch his mistake early enough to do some damage control, Darren says, "it will help him look better, [and] I want my boss to look good because if he looks good, then the rest of us are looking good."

Even when a truth-teller has intentions as good as Darren's, the reality is that organizations typically flinch from unwelcome facts. Whether in armies or businesses, the pressure keeps building on leaders to look good and achieve success. The pressure also makes them increasingly vulnerable to ambitious subordinates avid to promote their own careers even if they have to encourage their bosses to make disastrous mistakes.

For any leader, the temptation to ignore unpleasant truths is always there, and there will always be aye-aye people eager to help you do it. But the price can be devastating, as we have seen over and over in the recent litany of corporate scandals, failed mega-mergers, and collapsing hedge funds. Most, if not all, of them can be blamed on leaders whose wishful thinking was endorsed by the aye-aye chorus.

Fortunately, perhaps as a result of these disasters, we're seeing at least a temporary return to respect for the truth at big organizations. One encouraging sign comes from the Army, which is beginning a critical self-assessment of the miscues in Iraq to make sure they will never be repeated. For another example, recent reports indicate that major foundations, which once dismissed unsuccessful ventures as if they had never existed, are now conducting postmortems of their failures in an effort to find out what went wrong and avoid making the same mistakes again. After the Carnegie Foundation's ill-starred efforts to help Zimbabwe overhaul its constitution and its government, for instance, the foundation published a report that began, "This is the anatomy of a grant that failed." Similarly, the James Irvine Foundation publicly analyzed the shortcomings that doomed a $60 million afterschool program in California. "It just seems to me," said Irvine CEO James E. Canales, "that you aren't going to be credible if all you talk about is your successes." Such public assessments need to be done in business, routinely and often, so that lessons learned can be enshrined in future operating procedures.

It is plainly suicidal for any high-stakes leader to reject bad news as if it were a live hand grenade and treat its messenger like a traitor. The point of this chapter is that leaders in place or in training have an overwhelming incentive to encourage truth-telling by themselves and everyone who reports to them. Sure, honesty can be dangerous, but, in the long run, dishonesty always loses.

Here are some good ways to spread that message.

LET PEOPLE TELL THE ADMIRAL THE TRUTH.

I tried to encourage straight talk on *Benfold*, even when it seemed a bit risky. Certain admirals, for example, love to visit Navy ships and bathe their egos in what they perceive as the awe and admiration of the lower ranks. Few officers and fewer sailors dare to speak to the august visitors, much less raise problems that the admirals might help solve. So before any admiral's visit, I briefed my sailors on what the boss could do to improve their lives, and I encouraged them to ask questions.

To gauge the importance of visitors, we developed what we called the Scheeler Scale, named after our own Command Master Chief Bob Scheeler. The scale, graded one to ten, measured how much the visitor could help us and determined what level of service he or she would get. A ten was a big deal, meaning that all work stopped, the ship was cleaned thoroughly, and dress uniforms were the required attire. Dignitaries rated one would be allowed on the ship and given visitors' badges, but they could walk around by themselves. A five merited lunch in the wardroom with the officers, but a nine or ten meant lunch on the mess decks with the crew. The crew knew that if I really wanted to impress a dignitary, I would let him talk with the crew instead of the officers.

My crew's candor made some of our visitors cringe. One day, a new admiral arrived from the Pentagon to take over our battle group. We had a problem for him. In the late 1990s, San Diego rents were soaring while Navy housing allowances remained flat. Affordable housing near the Navy base was so scarce that, between voyages, some of my sailors had to commute nearly 100 miles to be with their families. My sailors duly asked the admiral why housing allowances were not rising to match rents.

The admiral bridled and insisted that rents were, in fact, dropping. Yeah, right—rents were dropping as housing costs soared. The admiral was either lying or hopelessly out of touch. After that, no one believed a word he said. Back in my office, the admiral accused me of provoking the crew to embarrass him. "You shouldn't get them riled up like this!" he yelled. Then he turned to his new aide, a San Diego–based officer named Dimitri: "Your rent isn't going up, right?"

It was a time for bravery. "Well, sir," Dimitri said, "it just went up 21 percent." Go, Dimitri!

MAKE TRUTH-TELLING YOUR OWN PERSONAL PREROGATIVE.

As the second son in a family-owned business, Michael Bleier had never given any thought to what constituted strong leadership and how to define a company's goals. He grew up in a command-and-control world where his father was the supremely competent, hard-nosed, strong-willed boss who ruled everything. No one questioned him; no one crossed him. And when Michael's brother took the reins of Able Distributors, he picked up where their father had left off.

Then, after twelve or so years of hiding away in a pleasant little niche he had carved for himself scouting out more energy-efficient products, Michael started to take an interest in managing the business. Encouraged by my friend Marc Jacobson, he began to see the necessity of having a leader who could define a company's mission and, as he puts it, "make it bigger than just selling a furnace." Michael's goal was to change Able from a nice, family-owned business into a great business that just happens to be run by a family. And, as I could have guessed, there were plenty of yes-men ready to flatter the boss in order to keep their seat at the family table. But Michael was ready for them.

"In almost any business, [telling] the truth seems to be the hardest thing" for people to do, he says. But by acknowledging his own fallibility and openly asking for help, Michael was able to keep the yes-men at bay. "Guys, I'm forty years old," he told his employees. "I kind of know what I'm doing, but I certainly haven't written any books on it. So let's work on [building a great business] together. I need your help. What do you think?"

Besides asking questions and owning up to making his own mistakes, Michael is all for crafting conversations with employees that are designed to drill into their heads the company's mission and culture, a big part of which is that his people "are paid to be truthful to each other and to customers."

"I don't pay everybody to love each other," he says, "but I do pay everybody to work together effectively [to achieve] superior products, superior service, and superior profitability." And the way Michael sees it, telling the truth is what it's all about—starting at the top: "First, be truthful yourself," is Michael Bleier's advice to any leader who aspires to great things. It is working for him at Able Distributors, and it will work for you no matter what line of work you're in.

NEVER LET PEOPLE KNOW WHAT YOU WANT TO HEAR—THEY'LL TELL YOU.

I learned a lot about making sure I got the truth when I was working for Defense Secretary William Perry. When he told people to study something, he never gave them a hint what he thought the answer might be. Because if he did, he knew the aye-aye chorus would come back with only a list of the reasons why he was right. Perry also understood that when the senior person in a room reveals what he's inclined to do, the others will jump to tell him it's a great idea and how lucky they are to be working for such a wise man. So when Perry was being briefed, he never indicated which way he might be leaning. After the briefer finished, Perry would summarize the facts and ask if he'd missed anything. If the briefer said no, Perry would briefly recount the options, with all their pros and cons, and ask again if he'd left anything out. Only then would he say, such and such is what we'll do. This guaranteed an open and honest airing of ideas and options.

WHEN THERE'S A PROBLEM, FIRST ASK HOW LONG PEOPLE HAVE KNOWN ABOUT IT.

I often say that bad news doesn't improve with age. When something went wrong on *Benfold*, I wanted to know it right away. Even if the bad-news bearers didn't have a plan to fix the problem, I didn't give them a hard time. If they told me they didn't have a plan but were working on one, I'd say fine—and maybe make a suggestion. But my first question was always, "How long have you known about this?"

That question tripped up an officer who failed to mention that his sonar equipment hadn't been working for two weeks. He wasn't maliciously hiding the problem; he was just a very talented officer who thought he could fix the equipment himself. But when he finally told me about the problem, we were heading out to sea for an exercise with the carrier battle group, and because his sonar wasn't working, we had to drop out of the exercise. It was the only commitment we missed during my tour as captain.

"How long have you known about it?" I inquired. "Two weeks," he said. I asked him how on earth he thought I could remedy the now-embarrassing equipment breakdown at this late date. Had he told me earlier, I barked, we could have called in experts, gotten new parts, or replaced what was broken. But when I don't know that something's broken, I can't help fix it. Because he hadn't told me the news, he had taken away all my options and left us dead in the water.

After this officer's dressing-down, everyone on *Benfold* knew there was only one correct answer to "How long have you known?" In very short order, no one was hiding problems. That question is one of the best management tools I know, and I recommend it to any leader who doesn't want to be blindsided. It's simple and direct, and an untruthful response is usually easy to spot.

DELIVER THE WORST NEWS YOURSELF WITHOUT DELAY, PAINFUL AS IT MAY BE.

The worst news anyone ever had to tell me on *Benfold* was that we had breached security. The job fell to Dave Hallisey, the department head of operations, and it wasn't a good day for him. He knew my reaction would be: "How could you allow this to happen?"

The breach occurred in the communications shack, which is really the security vault where all the ship's communications are handled. Over the years, as coding has become more sophisticated, the system has evolved so that codes can be changed on a daily or even hourly basis, and a new code can be downloaded over a phone line or the airwaves. To keep them secure, the ironclad rules are that at least two people have to be in the communications shack at all times, and personal computers are always strictly forbidden.

We had broken both rules. One of the two radiomen on duty had gone off to breakfast, leaving the other, known as something of a goofball, by himself. Worse, he had his computer and was reading and sending personal e-mail over the phone lines. He could easily have sent the coding material to anyone in the world. Potentially, this was a major breach of security that could have jeopardized the country and cost millions of dollars to fix.

A similar incident occurred when I was communications officer on *Albert David*. The department head wanted to cover it up, but my chief, Bob Dooley, said no, this was serious, and if the department head didn't take action, Bob would go to the captain. Chief Dooley forced the officer to do the right thing.

Needing no prompting, Dave Hallisey told me about our breach within half an hour of finding out. And at noon, I went to tell the commodore, my own face as ashen as Dave's had been.

The commodore was far less upset than I was. He figured, correctly as it turned out, that this breach smacked more of goofball behavior than espionage. We persuaded the radioman to waive his rights, and we searched his computer. His outgoing e-mail showed no trace of the codes or any other contraband. I reduced the thoughtless sailor's rank without delay, informed him of his deficiencies, and sent him to counseling.

Long after the incident was over, Dave and I still got chills just thinking about that day. But we agreed that promptly making a clean breast of it, and getting the input of sometimes wiser heads like our commodore's, saved everyone a lot of added aggravation and ulcer-producing worry.

RESIST THE IMPULSE TO PLEASE.

By and large, I had no trouble getting my junior sailors to tell the truth. They had little or no experience in the Navy and weren't accustomed to a system where senior officers wanted aye-aye men and women. But the older officers who had been around for a while had some trouble adjusting to my ways.

Dave Hallisey, for instance, had been the aide to a three-star admiral who had to be told what he wanted to hear, and I sometimes thought Dave was continuing that approach with me. As the operations department head, he basically ran the ship but also worked with the admiral's staff to schedule the jobs *Benfold* was assigned to do.

One of the things the admiral had to do was provide ships for what we called DLQs—deck landing qualifications—for helicopter pilots, who would practice landings and takeoffs from the moving ship. The job was monotonous, you had to stay on a steady course and speed, and the ship couldn't do anything else constructive while the DLQs were going on. The exercises came out of our training time, but we couldn't train.

Early in my command, we were assigned about a year's worth of DLQs in a month, and I was furious about it. So Dave, wanting to please me, used his considerable diplomatic skills to conspire with the admiral's staff to get other assignments and no more DLQs. The problem with Dave's solution was that DLQs do carry some benefits. Each member of the flight-deck crew gets $150 of extra pay, for instance, for a minimum number of DLQs every month. I didn't want to deprive the crew of the extra cash, so the trick was to get the minimum number of DLQs, but no more.

Finally, Dave figured out that if he proactively volunteered in advance to do the required minimum number of DLQs, the crew would get the extra pay and the admiral wouldn't hit us with any additional DLQs. Everyone would be happy.

SHOW YOU CARE BY SHARING THE BLUNT TRUTH, BUT BE RESPECTFUL.

Command Master Chief Scheeler was known for giving me facts I sometimes wished I didn't have to hear, but he always maintained the utmost respect for my authority. I could either accept his advice or reject it, but his response was always the same: "Yes, sir." After which he accepted my decision as if it were his own and went out the door determined to do his job and his duty, no matter what—and that meant supporting the guy who had the ultimate responsibility for the ship's well-being: me. Scheeler encouraged the chief petty officers under his supervision to do the same for him. He worked hard to keep the lines of communication open by bringing the chiefs together in the mess whenever an issue of general importance came to his attention. And he was determined not to come across as the ultimate decision maker, making it a point to seek the advice of those who worked for him.

I've never met a manager more committed to straight talk than Aflac's Teresa White. She supervises a workforce of more than 3,000 people, broken up into several departments. There's no point in being timid when directly communicating to employees. "I want my team members to know that I have their best interest in mind. So, I believe in being forthcoming when providing feedback. It's the right thing to do," Teresa says. Indeed, wanting to be respected for her honesty, she is candid to the point of bluntness in dealing with her people. To enforce Aflac's dress code, for instance, Teresa will stop an employee in the hall and ask, cheerfully but directly: "Why are you wearing that? You know you're not supposed to wear that here." Teresa thinks her exceedingly direct approach works because she truly respects her staffers. "People have told me that I get away with saying things that nobody else can say," she told me, "and people don't get offended."

If an employee is not performing up to par, Teresa points out the problems and offers training or other help in overcoming them. If nothing works and there is no alternative to firing the employee, she combines empathy and unrelenting frankness in the final interview.

Teresa reviews the shortcomings and the help the staffer has requested and received from her, and lays out the now-inevitable consequences. She doesn't offer a shoulder to cry on, but she does give the soon-to-be ex-employee a chance to determine how the termination will be explained to colleagues. "I like to leave people with their dignity intact," she says.

Teresa is also a reliable source of candid advice for employees who want to get ahead and feel they aren't advancing fast enough. "When someone calls and wants to get on my calendar because they want to know why they didn't get a job, I'm excited, because I get an opportunity to help them understand why and coach them about what they can do about it," she says.

In one case, a bright young woman with a very strong résumé came to Teresa wanting to know why she kept missing out on good jobs. At first, Teresa was baffled: "I'm looking at her credentials, and she's got all the boxes checked—degrees, certification, experience, you name it." But as they talked, it became clear why the woman never got beyond the initial interviews. "She talked extremely fast," Teresa recalls, and used vernacular grammar, saying "they is," for instance, instead of "they are."

At this point, looking the young woman in the eye, Teresa gave it to her straight: "I think I know why you're not getting these jobs. You may not like what I'm going to say, but you asked me a question and I'm going to tell you the truth." Teresa told the woman her speech was rushed and her grammar poor. She advised her to slow down and think before she spoke.

The young woman was shocked and dismayed, and reached for a tissue. "It's not an easy conversation to have, especially with people who really, really want success," Teresa told me. "She had the credentials; she just wanted to know what she needed to do to get the job."

"Is this too hard for you right now?" Teresa asked. "Do you not want to do this?" No, I want to go on, the woman said. So Teresa offered to act as pre-interviewer the next time she sought a new position. A few days later, the young woman let Teresa know that her advice had been well received. "I'm practicing!" she said proudly.

KEEP INFORMATION MOVING IN A TWO-WAY FLOW FROM TOP TO BOTTOM.

In my first month on the job as captain of *Benfold*, I found out that, apparently, the sailors took a very dim view of my predecessor's perceived penchant for saying only what the admiral wanted to hear. The perception among the sailors was that the captain cared only about advancing his own career. I didn't know whether they were right or not, but that view may have caused them to distrust the captain.

Now, I had no way of knowing the ship's dynamics before coming aboard, but it didn't take long for me to get an inkling of the captain-crew relationship. As the man left the ship accompanied by his family, the crew cheered when his departure was announced. I felt embarrassed by the sailors' lack of respect and wanted to know what had prompted it. So I called Command Master Chief Scheeler to my cabin to get the lowdown. Here's what he told me:

"Captain, I was standing out on the flight deck watching the sailors pitch the tent, put out the 300 chairs for the dignitaries, paint over rust, and doing whatever it took to get the ship looking good for the ceremony when your predecessor came up to me and asked how I would rate the morale of the crew." Afraid to tell the captain the truth—that, on a scale of one to ten, the master chief would rate morale at one—he instead said four or five.

But guess what the departing captain said? "I disagree. I would say it was an eight-and-a-half or a nine," he told Scheeler. Talk about being in the dark. Here was a leader who had no real clue about what his people thought of him. That doesn't mean my predecessor was a bad guy; just that no one was telling him the truth, and surely his command suffered for it.

In working with an automobile sales group, I've learned that mismatched perceptions can hurt profits. This group has proven data showing that dealerships with the highest sales volume and greatest profitability also have owners, customers, and employees who all share the same perceptions about the dealership's products, service, attention to customers, and other performance measures. The worst performers are dealerships with the biggest mismatches in perception.

The lesson here is that when people are afraid to tell you the truth—for whatever reason—you've created a barrier that keeps you from getting the best out of your people. And when everyone, from top to bottom, is privy to correct information that enables them to form valid assessments, the business or the ship will have a better chance of hitting on all twelve cylinders.

DON'T RUN AGROUND ON DETAILS.

On *Benfold*, I once had to give some very straight talk to John Wade. He was the officer I told you about in Chapter 1 who got off to a good start on his first ship by learning all the jobs his sailors had to do. His method helped him to become an expert on everything for which he was responsible. Unfortunately, that was the wrong lesson for his new job.

John came to *Benfold* as one of the ship's five department heads, which in his case meant he was responsible for all the weapons systems. He came aboard in 1997 on the very day we shipped out for the Persian Gulf. Two days later, the fire-control sprinkler system in one of the ship's munitions magazines broke down. The breakdown presented a real danger, because a fire in a magazine could sink the ship and kill everyone onboard. To my knowledge, this has never happened to a ship in peacetime, so while the system needed to be repaired quickly, there was no need to go to general quarters over it.

But John went with what he knew: He consulted the technical manuals and had his men explain how the system worked and what the options were for repairing it. So far, so good. After an hour of getting his ducks in a row, he came to me with all the manuals and drawings and explained the problem. He spent twenty minutes drilling into it and showing me how we could bypass the broken valve for a temporary fix. When I asked if he was finished, and he answered, "Yes, sir," I told him: "John, you are going to fail as a department head."

He was shocked to his core; he thought he had done the right thing. But I reminded him that the technicians were trained to understand the minute details of the system. As a department head, he was supposed to understand the problem and the risk in broad terms, explain it clearly to the captain, tell how he meant to fix it, and say whether he needed any help. "You can do that in less than two minutes," I said. "Both you and I have overwhelming jobs. If we get bogged down in the minutiae that our people and division officers are supposed to know, we won't have time to see the big picture." Going through the drill with his people to find out whom he could trust was a good thing. But once John knew that he could depend on his go-to people, he needed to let them run, focusing his own attention on other areas that needed help.

It was a tough lesson to hear, but John was smart and caught on fast. And the bluntness of the message helped drive it home.

John Wade was probably my number one officer on the ship, and he had the ability to become a great captain, maybe even a three- or four-star admiral. He and I often talked on the bridge wing about my view of upper leadership and how he needed to prepare himself to think like an admiral or a corporate executive. Later, when he was commanding his own patrol craft, he turned a ship that had been in rough shape into one of the best. I'd wanted him to start seeing the bigger picture, and he learned the lesson well. As I write this book, John is preparing to take command of his own destroyer.

In business today, everyone seems so caught up in short-term problems that they can't take time to think about what the battlefield is going to look like three to five years down the road. If they don't have time to envision the future, they certainly won't have time to put the machinery in place to cope with it. And one of the biggest and most important obligations of business leaders is to train those who are coming up the ladder, so that they can leave their organizations in good hands. That's what I tried to get John Wade to think about. If you're caught up in all the minutiae, you'll miss the bigger picture.

ENCOURAGE MAVERICKS (TO A POINT).

Like me, Teresa White views straight talk as an essential, inescapable part of her leadership role. In return, she expects unvarnished truths from her people. She tells team members, "If you bring it to the table and you never share it, then, well, I'm down one person." She reminds her employees that she isn't all-seeing or all-knowing, and she actually demands opinions that differ from hers: "If you see that something we're doing is going to send us off a cliff, then, as a team member, it's your responsibility to let me know. Please don't allow me to fall off that cliff," she implores.

Even chronic naysayers are welcome on Teresa's teams, because she sees them as crucial contributors to any group. She says their concerns and objections are a check on overambitious plans and a speed bump for those who might too easily get carried away with them. "I use naysayers to tell myself, 'Hmmm, based on what they say, if I still want to go in this direction, I'm going to have to mitigate these issues with some strategies.'"

Balance is what Teresa is after. For every analytical person like herself, she believes, there needs to be a "motivator," someone who says, "Enough analysis paralysis; let's get moving!" For every naysayer, crossing arms and throwing up verbal roadblocks, there has to be a communicator drawing information from the negativity.

You might suppose that Teresa would keep to herself the roles she applies to her team members, but you would be wrong. She is only too happy to tell visitors to a team meeting that "Jason is my analytical person, Blake is my communicator, Kevin my naysayer, and Tammy my . . . well, as soon as it's out of my mouth, she's doing it, so I know I better not say it until I'm sure I want it done." Employees wear their designated hats comfortably and with good humor, because they understand that Teresa values each role and respects them all for what they bring to the table. They see her honesty for what it is, and they repay it with loyal, dedicated commitment to the job.

It's human nature to look for approval for the thing you want to do, and it's a universal trait for people to tell their leaders what the leaders want to hear. By the same token, unpleasant truths are often handled with sugarcoating, or even flat-out lying to pretend they're not there. Most of the time, that's the way we handle social life.

But in business as in the Navy, such tactics are far too costly to be tolerated. A real leader learns ways to promote and reward truth-telling, demands honesty from his or her crew, and never punishes messengers with bad news. And it's only on that understanding that any leader can achieve the goal of the next chapter: to create a truly unified workforce with a common set of objectives and a well-honed way to reach them.

CHAPTER 4

ALL HANDS ON DECK

UNIFYING A CREW

WHEN I TOOK COMMAND OF *BENFOLD*, IT WAS A SPECTAC-
ular fighting machine, one of the Navy's most advanced
guided-missile destroyers. With four gas turbine engines power-
ing this billion-dollar baby, I could kick it up to thirty-one knots,
nearly thirty-five miles an hour, throwing up a huge rooster tail
in her wake. The radar system could track an object the size of a
bird from fifty miles away, and it could lay down more firepower
than the entire Navy was capable of in World War II. All *Benfold*
lacked was a unified crew. What she had was 310 sullen, unhappy
men and women working at cross-purposes with one another and
making my ship a fractious and thoroughly miserable place.

Sarah Garner, who joined the ship as a combat fire control
technician a few months before I arrived, recalls that many of the
sailors literally hid out in inconspicuous places where they could

avoid doing any work while supposedly on duty. So embedded was the system that the best hideouts were actually reserved, like tables at a popular restaurant. "That's Pete's hiding place," Sarah was told at one point. "You can't go in there."

In business today, there can be no hiding places. And neither can there be lone rangers who refuse to collaborate with the rest of the team. Unity, respect, and collaboration are the watchwords in the modern business community. Success in a rapid-fire, globalized world demands that everyone pull together, and when they do, performance skyrockets.

I've written before about some of the techniques I used to bring together *Benfold*'s 310 dispirited individuals into one first-rate crew. I communicated regularly with the sailors and their families through the public address system and the ship's newsletter, and I wrote personal letters to spouses and parents whenever a crew member had done something praiseworthy. I tried to make working on *Benfold* as much fun as possible, with parties, competitions, and games to liven up the routine. And I rewarded dedication and good teamwork with every tool at my disposal—from praise and public recognition to bigger assignments and more responsibility.

One unifying tactic that truly set us apart from other Navy commands was our unusual outreach to young officers who hadn't even been commissioned yet. As noted earlier, we sent them our packet of *Benfold* gear—the hat, the T-shirt, the bumper sticker—as soon as we learned they were coming to our ship. So, unlike their fellow midshipmen at Annapolis or graduating ROTC students at various colleges and universities, our new officers could proudly show off the visible symbols of *Benfold*'s welcoming atmosphere before their friends had ever heard a word from their own ships. We gave them a strong desire to be part of our community right from the start.

But perhaps my most life-changing move to promote unity and collaboration came on my second day as *Benfold*'s commanding officer, when I laid out a radical new rule for the ship's five major department heads. They had to stop backbiting, competing, and sabotaging each other, and start collaborating and cooperating. The rivalry among department heads is traceable to a simple fact of Navy life: The commander of a ship is expected to rank his department heads once a year, and only the one or two at the top will be considered for command of a ship. For the rest, their Navy careers are effectively finished; they may stay in the service, but they will never again be promoted and will have to retire after twenty years.

This system isn't all bad; far from it. In fact, the Navy's selection process is the fairest way I can think of to identify people for promotion. It works like this: You get your annual evaluation; you're ranked accordingly; and you also get letter grades. The senior officer doing the ranking may try to be kind by giving all his people straight A's. But being nice to underachievers means he'll only end up harming the outstanding performers.

You see, each reporting senior officer's grading average is recorded over the years. By keeping track of that historic average, a commanding officer can send a clear signal to a selection board that this officer is an above-average performer by bestowing a grade well above his usual marks. But if all the marks given over the years are high, the officer deprives himself of a way to reward the cream of the crop.

The Navy selection boards have nine members, usually headed by an admiral. Everyone on the board is senior to the person being considered for promotion, and each member reviews a candidate's record, diving deep into the person's background and qualifications to assess strengths, failings, and future potential. After a candidate's record is discussed, each board member casts a secret vote on a covered keypad, which reflects the member's degree of confidence in the candidate—100 percent, 75 percent, 50 percent, 25 percent, or zero. The average score then appears on the screen.

By and large, the Navy's promotion system is as searching and objective as human selection can be, and no board member can unduly influence anyone else. (Corporations should consider this system as a way to improve on their promotion processes.) Nonetheless, the system ensures that competition among department heads will be intense and sometimes bitter, because each tries to shine at his colleagues' expense. It gets so nasty that some departments won't lend a hand when another department needs help.

When I served on a previous ship, the backstabbing was furious. One fellow department head, in particular, would openly denigrate the other department heads in meetings with the captain, and would do everything he could to undermine them. They weren't going to get any cooperation from his department if he could block it. That attitude filtered down to his people as well. As a result, that ship was just as dysfunctional as *Benfold* was when I took command.

The paradox of the Navy's promotion system is that it's incorruptible in terms of fairness but corrupt in its effect on morale. It drives officers apart rather than together. It stems from some hoary notion that warriors must be conditioned to fight each other, the better to fight the enemy. That's fine for gladiators, fighter pilots, and other lone wolves. But it's no way to build a unit of people who depend on one another's brains and backup to prevail against mortal danger. Imagine applying the Navy promotion system to a life raft loaded with shipwrecked officers in a sea churning with hungry sharks. Enough said.

This chapter takes the pragmatic view that mindless rivalry leads to backstabbing, an ethos of every man for himself, and probable unit failure when danger threatens. In other words, dumb competition actually makes organizations weaker. Conversely, smart collaboration makes them stronger. If I had just one lesson to pass on from my *Benfold* experience, it would be this: Nothing beats the power of unifying disparate people, of showing them the magic of working with and for each other instead of against each other. Quite simply, the first law of leadership in today's world is to give people irresistible incentives to collaborate for a purpose that enhances everyone.

Striving for that effect became my *Benfold* priority. Accordingly, my crew and I improvised many unifying techniques, the best of which follow.

YOU DON'T HAVE TO BE AN ADMIRAL.

All through my Navy career, I had accepted rivalry as a necessary evil. I was as driven as anyone else. I was the second youngest midshipman in the class of 1982 at the Naval Academy. It was driven into us from Day One that you had to make admiral; anything less would mean failure. So I had to get the best fitness reports so the Navy would deem me worthy to be an admiral. I was one of only three who got promoted to lieutenant commander two years ahead of the usual schedule. I got hired by Defense Secretary

Perry, arguably the most prestigious job for any commander, and I was the first in my class to be promoted to commander, so I was senior to all my classmates. I just had to be number one. If I didn't make admiral, I would consider myself a failure.

There were two events that changed my attitude and turned my life around. The first came while I was working for Dr. Perry. In my first few months there, I was miserable. I was the newcomer and I had to prove myself. At senior levels in government, you have to prove yourself trustworthy before you're allowed into the inner circle. So for the first months, I got only grunt work to do, basically paper shuffling. I was supposed to decide which issues would go to Dr. Perry.

But when I sent my recommendations to my boss, Perry's senior military aide and a two-star Army general, he rejected 90 percent of them. I was so frustrated that I felt like crying behind my closed door because I seemed so insignificant in my own eyes.

Then I remembered Chief Dooley's advice and tried to put myself in the general's shoes. By analyzing what he did with my recommendations, I began to learn what was important and how he thought. I got permission to sit in on some meetings and learned how Dr. Perry ran them. When the general's son came down with a rare illness, I sat in for him for almost two months. I was working eighty to ninety hours a week, sometimes around the clock, and I didn't do the job perfectly. However, I never screwed up completely. When the general came back, I overheard him ask Dr. Perry how I had done. Perry said, "Paul, I consider you and Mike interchangeable now."

It was no compliment for a two-star general to be called equivalent to me, and he wasn't happy. But for me it was a kind of benediction. From that day forward, promotion wasn't the goal.

I had been doing the work of a two-star general, the same job Colin Powell—one of my great role models—had when he was a two-star. I had my success. I no longer had to make admiral since I now had affirmation that I could do admiral-level work. In business, life-changing validations don't come from a year-end bonus. They often come from seemingly inconsequential statements from those we respect and admire the most.

MISSION: COLLABORATION.

The second event that changed my life came on the day I took command of *Benfold*. In *It's Your Ship*, I told the story—partially recounted in the preceding chapter—of how my predecessor was raucously jeered off the ship by a crew that seemingly had come to hate his guts. That was a defining moment. In all honesty, if that hadn't happened, I might have gone on tolerating all the hypercompetitive rivalry, bickering, and backstabbing that had been such a part of my Navy career.

But I decided then and there that success in this job meant excellence, which would actually be undermined by competition for promotion. How could I do my best? How could I make the ship the best? How could I keep my crew from getting injured or killed because not everyone aboard was doing his or her best? I had learned that what drives performance isn't rivalry but unity. I had to unite the whole crew and make everyone row in the same direction.

So the day after I took command, I called the department heads to a meeting. There was the head of operations, who runs the combat information center and directs the ship in battle. There were two heads of combat systems, because the systems are so big and complex, and one each for engineering, navigation, and administration and supply. And I gave them a very simple message: Collaboration was to be a top priority, I said, and when it came time to rank them, one of my main criteria would be how well they supported the other departments. Anyone who refused to cooperate would be ranked at the bottom.

But I also made them a promise: "Look, you guys know I have to rank you and not all of you are going to be considered for command." If they weren't ranked at the top but had done a good job, I guaranteed that I would do whatever I could when they left the ship to help them get whatever jobs they wanted in whatever place. "And if you're planning on leaving the Navy," I said, "I'll get you a job that helps you prepare for that transition."

After that, the department heads saw that it was in their interest to cooperate. And in hindsight, if I could point to one thing that made *Benfold* excel, it was the departments working together as a team. I would see the heads of the five departments in the officers' mess, working out issues among themselves because they didn't want to have to come to me to resolve a problem.

It was that kind of coordination that made it possible to get the most out of what we called the PB4T, the planning board for training. The department heads and the top program assistants met once a week with the executive officer to plan every minute of the following week, taking into account long-range projects extending as much as six months out. For instance, if the engineers needed time to practice hazard control, we scheduled it so as not to interfere with, say, a combat systems exercise requiring some of the same space or equipment. If a recertification period was coming up, we knew that all departments would have to cover their bases in the next six weeks, so we roughed in a schedule ahead of time.

There was a remarkable amount of give-and-take in the planning, with really generous cooperation that went beyond the letter of the law. In certification, for example, the engineers are judged in part on how clean their space is. Since that space includes the bilges, they have to be cleaned—a filthy, low-tech job. The engineers surely could have done it, but it would have been $10-an-hour work for people who could have been doing $100-an-hour work practicing emergency procedures or tuning up the ship's turbines. So, without complaint (okay, maybe a little), the other departments lent sailors to clean the bilges.

And when department heads had projects that required the best-trained people, I made sure their colleagues sent their best, not just people they'd gladly get rid of. My directive inflicted some pain, but it meant that high-priority projects got tackled by the first team. In the end, it worked to everyone's benefit.

Darren Barton, my Tomahawk technician who is now a chief petty officer, tells me that the Navy as a whole is starting to be more like a corporation. Accordingly, he sees more emphasis on cooperation and collaboration among departments. "The way I work with my guys," Darren says, "is we take care of our own shop and the division and once that is good, then we help out the department. When the department is in good shape, then we help the whole command. We have to make sure our part of the machine is working properly before we can effectively help others with their problems." The ultimate goal is to perfect the Navy itself.

Once the team concept is embedded and people stop thinking only of perfecting and protecting their little niches, it's easier to see what else needs doing. Better yet, people come to realize that when the whole ship—or the whole Navy—is performing well, it works to everyone's advantage.

A UNIFIED TEAM IS A BOON FOR CUSTOMERS, TOO.

In a move reminiscent of my command to *Benfold* department heads to stop backbiting, competing, and sabotaging one another, Michael Bleier at Able Distributors constantly tells his people that treating one's workmates with respect and kindness translates into better treatment of customers. And it makes sense when you consider that the energy formerly expended on jockeying to get back at or ahead of a fellow employee is freed up for much more productive uses, like taking the best possible care of customers.

Michael readily admits that he himself used to think only of how he might fight his way through the system to accomplish his own work to serve his customers and his priorities. As far as he was concerned, it was every man for himself—no matter how it affected the company and its customers overall.

But since what he calls his "awakening" to the demands of real leadership, he attempts to embody the idea that good treatment of everyone by everyone else is a noble cause. "It's like servant-leadership," he says. And he encourages his employees to think and talk often about how best to achieve this goal. It's a theme that runs through every segment of the company's operations. "What's interesting," Michael points out, "is that now the culture polices itself to a large degree in a good way. We are all holding each other to higher standards."

When I asked him for specifics, he told me that, in the past, his company was compartmentalized, and the guys in the purchasing department controlled everything. They made sure merchandise was purchased, they oversaw where it was sent, and they even had a hand in how products were stocked. So, naturally, if anything at all went wrong, they got blamed, which helped no one—especially not the company's customers.

Say a contractor came in to order ten items but only seven of them were in stock. The counter person would automatically say, "Oh, those guys in purchasing, they screwed us over. They are really bad. I'm sorry, but there's really nothing I can do." In short, nobody had to take responsibility for any foul-ups; they just pushed the blame off on the purchasing department. And with no one accepting responsibility, none of the problem spots were getting fixed.

These days, the purchasing department no longer runs the whole show and the counter guy isn't just manning the storefront; he's now an inside salesperson. With the new division of responsibilities, Able's employees have stopped playing the blame game, Michael told me, and they have started protecting one another. "Now, if we only have seven out of the ten items the contractor needs, the response from the counter person is 'Wow, what can we do to make this better? Are there other items we can substitute? Can we direct you to another place? Can we deliver the items to you later?'" No longer can a weak link be used as an excuse to bash another part of the company, Michael says, because the newly unified Able has strengthened the weak links.

GIVE EVERYONE A CHANCE TO
STEER THE SHIP.

Until Bill Walsh changed the climate, the National Football League had much the same sort of institutionalized backstabbing among coaches that the Navy did. Head coaches would try to hang on to their assistants, keeping them away from media attention and discouraging them from interviewing for better jobs with other teams. The assistants were left to contend bitterly for the few promotions available on their own teams.

Earlier in his career, Walsh says, when he was trying to advance from a job as assistant with the Cincinnati Bengals, the team's founder and coach, Paul Brown, actually tried to blackball him. Walsh wrote in his book that Brown called around the league to make sure no one offered Walsh a head coach's job. So he left the NFL for Stanford University, coaching the college players to two successive bowl games before the San Francisco 49ers hired Walsh in 1979 to salvage a team that had managed only two wins in a sixteen-game season.

In San Francisco, Walsh reversed the NFL's notorious pattern. Always generous to his assistants, he gave them credit for their work, let them talk to reporters, and actively helped when they were looking for advancement. "I've never known any coach more tireless in his efforts to help the people around him," one of his former assistants told *Sports Illustrated*. "I can never repay Bill, but part of his legacy is that I feel compelled to do it for other coaches, and I think we all feel the same way." As a result, the league is heavily populated with Walsh protégés who are now head coaches—and, not incidentally, Walsh had no problem finding top candidates to replace those who left.

In business today, for all the reengineering that has gone on now for two decades, all too many companies still have departments that operate in a self-contained manner, and too many executives have no idea how to tear down the walls. I recently talked to an insurance company that was built on a series of mergers; its various divisions were still operating as if they were separate companies, bidding against each other to sell policies to the same customers. It was both embarrassing to the company and damaging to the bottom line.

The problem should have been easy enough to solve by simply aligning the divisions' economic interests so that they would cooperate rather than compete. One way to accomplish the alignment would have been to assign one of two traditionally competitive divisions the lead role in attracting customers while giving the other division a cut of the profit on the deal as compensation for collaboration. But, according to the chief operating officer, the issue had never turned up on his radar screen. And, as far as I know, the company is still trying to figure it out.

FORGET KEEPING UP APPEARANCES.

In business just as in the Navy, too many people spend too much time keeping up appearances and not enough time concentrating on delivering excellence. On one of the ships where I served, a department head sat in his stateroom every day until both the captain and the XO had left the ship. Even though he was done with his work at 4:30, he'd sit there into the night with the door shut reading a paperback book, just to prove that he was on the job.

I always worked hard, but when my work was done, I went home. I wasn't there to sit at a desk and look good. Even though I was known as the department head who always left first—a no-no—I still got good rankings, which just proves how needless it is to put on a show.

It's foolish to work endless hours even if Navy conventions demand it. The workday at sea is a 24/7 operation, which means that people have to stand watch around the clock. If you're on the midnight-to–6:00 a.m. watch, you're supposed to go right on working until 5:00 p.m. There were days when I walked around like a zombie, without the mental acuity to decide anything.

So one of the first things I did on *Benfold* was to tell my officers they wouldn't be graded on how late they stayed every night, nor would I be checking their bunks at sea; they could take a nap if they got tired. No one had to keep up appearances. I just wanted them to do their jobs the best they could and to be mentally alert at all times.

MAKE LIFE BETTER FOR YOUR CREW.

From my first days aboard *Benfold*, I looked for ways to improve morale. I wanted the ship's store stocked with snacks and items that my sailors would relish. I wanted meals they would want to eat, movie nights with giveaway popcorn, flight-deck picnics, Friday-night happy hours without alcohol but with bar-type snacks, and "slider days," when the mess served hamburgers and hot dogs. All these lifestyle improvements involved a good deal of organizing and some creative budgeting, but my supply officer

Dave Devlin and his assistant, George Lynett, were enthusiastic about the job.

One small example was the issue of clothing the crew could wear when on liberty. The sailors wanted to wear civilian clothes, jeans and T-shirts and the like, but the ship's laundry wasn't up to cleaning them; we had the equipment but not enough workers. Some sailors with buddies working in the laundry were getting their civilian clothes washed, which led to complaints about favoritism. It was becoming a morale issue.

So Dave and George called for junior volunteers from each of the ship's five divisions, and they were trained to use the washers, the dryers, and the big industrial pressing machines to clean everybody's civilian clothes. The volunteers became heroes in their divisions, and the laundry crew wasn't being overworked.

I became a hero of sorts to many crew members who were fed up with hearing Jimmy Buffett's "Cheeseburger in Paradise" blasted over the PA system every Wednesday during lunch. Wednesday was designated as Slider Day, as I noted earlier, and in the beginning, Buffett's song seemed to go with Slider Day like, well, cheese on a burger. But after one too many repetitions, it was just annoying. When I authorized a raffle that entitled the winner to use the CD as target practice off the fantail, all but diehard Buffett fans cheered. The raffle was a huge success, and we donated the money to the MWR (the morale, welfare, and recreation fund).

The ship's store was also a source of entertainment. Petty Officer Matt Blackman held sales on items the sailors enjoyed giving away whenever we were in a liberty port—things like baseball caps and cigarette lighters with the ship's name on them. When I discovered that the leftover items from the old regime included two cases of Old Spice shaving lotion, which were in about as much demand as buggy whips, I ordered George to get rid of them.

The Old Spice sale went on for a full day, promoted by a stream of funny announcements by George and Matt on the PA system. But the stuff wasn't moving very fast. We were heading for a liberty port that day, so I got on the microphone and announced that we weren't going in until the last bottle was gone. That did it.

The whole ship reeked of Old Spice during that liberty, and the crew thought the episode was hilarious. It was even funnier after we left port and George confessed that he had run across another case of the stuff in the storeroom. We had to put on yet another sale to get rid of that.

George Lynett, by the way, left the Navy to become a publisher in his family's newspaper business in Pennsylvania. He told me not long ago that he uses many of the management techniques he learned on *Benfold*: He interviews with all his people, schedules regular breakfasts and lunches with selected groups, thanks people publicly when they do well, and gives employees power with clearly defined limits.

George makes sure everyone understands the company's goals and values, and he constantly looks for examples of both excellent and substandard work. The best examples get actively and publicly praised; the worst get quietly fixed.

If imitation is the best form of flattery, I am both flattered and proud.

HAVE FUN WITH THE BORING JOBS.

I set up a continuing program to make all the work as much fun as possible for everyone onboard. When we were in the Persian Gulf, for instance, daytime refueling at sea was an exercise in parboiling as we steamed along slowly beside the tanker under the brutal Gulf sun. Since the sea was usually calm at night, we tried refueling after dark. It was less of an ordeal, and one sailor proposed making it entertaining for both crews by projecting music videos on the ship's rear bulkhead. That led to a laser light show. As we closed in on the tanker, we would blast the Olympic theme song on our PA system and shoot laser beams into the night sky, after which we played the music videos. It was quite an entertaining maneuver.

Soon, we added a live concert, with my talented navigator, K. C. Marshall, doing songs and impersonations with a karaoke machine. One night just before Christmas in 1997, we were refueling on one side of the tanker with the carrier *Nimitz* on the other side. Marshall impersonated Elvis Presley for nearly an hour, and his rendition of "Blue Christmas" was so touching that one of the officers on the *Nimitz*'s bridge was seen wiping away tears, overcome with missing his family.

We also played music to enliven such mundane chores as stowing away supplies, and I insisted on parties and entertainment as often as duty allowed. Before heading out to our assignment in the Gulf, I took aboard 100 cases of beer—to the consternation of Master Chief Scheeler and the executive officer, since drinking alcoholic beverages on a Navy ship is strictly forbidden except in rare circumstances. I had no exact plan to use the beer, but I knew it would come in handy.

Sure enough, at the end of our 100-day tour of duty, it looked like my sailors were going to be stuck on the ship for New Year's Eve, with no chance to celebrate on liberty ashore. So I hired a huge barge to meet us at an anchorage, ordered that the beer be chilled, and joined in the fun of a New Year's Eve cookout on our party barge, tied up alongside the still technically dry *Benfold*. Many of the sailors said it was the best New Year's Eve party they'd ever attended.

Darren Barton certainly hasn't forgotten that once-in-a-lifetime event. "We were anchored out in Bahrain," he recalls. "The only time we are allowed [to drink beer onboard] is if we've been out at sea for forty-five days straight. . . . No way would we be out forty-five days this time. We had the beer still coolin' down in the hold, so the captain got a barge. . . . At one end of the barge away from the ladder [up to *Benfold*], they set up coolers and drank beer on the barge. So, technically, it wasn't on the ship and, therefore, not violating any regulations. But we were able to have liberty and have a beer."

Years later, Sarah Garner told me how our entertainments had affected her morale and performance. "It just made working fun," she said. "It would keep people motivated and moving. The feeling was, 'Yes, we have to do this and it isn't always the best job in the world, but we're going to enjoy it.'"

BREAK UP LOGJAMS.

Since leaving the Navy, I've run across some intriguing techniques for unifying the crew, techniques I hadn't seen or even thought of before. Brian Scudamore, for example, likes to run his 1-800-

GOT-JUNK? business by consensus decisions. But when consensus can't be reached, one person on every team has been designated SPA—single-point accountable—and that member is empowered to break the logjam with a final decision.

Brian's business is a multimillion-dollar international franchising operation that he grew from a local trash-hauling company in Vancouver, British Columbia. It claims to be the biggest junk removal business in the world, with a brand built on Internet technology, scrupulously clean trucks, punctual operations, and well-trained, courteous, and uniformed drivers.

The operation is run from offices called "the Junktion" on Vancouver's waterfront, with a $1 million computer network handling calls for 330 franchise operators across Canada, the United States, and Australia. The youthful staffers are chosen for their zest, irreverence, and sense of fun—a combination that Brian relishes for a working atmosphere, but one that doesn't always lend itself to consensus.

Hence the SPA system, which Brian ran across when he was studying the franchise operations of what was then Mail Boxes Etc., since acquired by UPS.

To give an idea of how it works, Brian described a meeting at which a four-member team discussed whether to fire an employee. (Although 1-800-GOT-JUNK? takes pride in its low turnover, Brian emphasizes the importance of acting decisively when someone is not a good fit.) A majority soon agreed that the woman in question, who dealt directly with customers in the call center, lacked the energy and enthusiasm to do the job well. Her supervisor argued that she was "an incredibly nice and honest person, a team player, and incredibly loyal." Other team members agreed, but insisted that the point was irrelevant, because the woman was not up to the job and never would be. Eventually, the SPA member announced the team decision: The woman would have to go.

The SPA leader asked the woman's supervisor if he understood why the decision had been made. He did. The leader then asked if the supervisor agreed with the decision. Not 100 percent, he replied, but he assured the SPA leader that he would support the decision as a team member fully committed to carrying it out.

When individual members of a team know they can state their views freely and be sure their opinions will receive serious consideration, that knowledge fosters a group spirit and mutual loyalty that can overcome disagreements. Even absent the SPA structure, I've seen this work time and again on *Benfold*. We are also obligated to support fully all decisions, even if we don't agree with them 100 percent.

DON'T BLAME PEOPLE; BLAME THE SYSTEM.

Brian Scudamore's operation has another unifying technique that I've come to admire. It's known in the Junktion as "Huddle," and it begins every morning when the first person to notice that the clock has reached 10:55 yells out, at lung-straining volume, "Huddle!" At that, all sixty-two employees, from the newest call-center operator to Brian himself, have just sixty seconds to get to the meeting.

The Huddle starts with the question, "Who's got good news?" There is apt to be some personal news that is greeted with cheers ("Our first baby is expected in December," Brian himself reported in a Huddle). But most of the reports concern the business, something like: "Our franchise partner in Denver just landed a 140-

truckload job." The talk then turns to current issues or details about previous issues: progress on a refined design for the company's standard dump truck, perhaps, or extended comment about the thirteen large porcelain Buddhas and prosthetic leg carted away by a franchisee during the week.

The last question at every Huddle is this: "Are there any missing systems or key frustrations?" Sometimes there are, sometimes there aren't. Either way, it's fine, because nothing personal is involved. 1-800-GOT-JUNK?'s corporate culture doesn't seek to attach problems to any individual or team. The mantra of the organization is that "people don't fail, systems do."

As Brian told me, "We do not have a culture of blame. When something goes wrong, we just try to get to the root of the problem. It's not that someone's stupid. It's usually that there was a missing system, and we have to prevent it from happening again."

I would add one more thing: When systems do fail, a leader should start fixing them by looking into a mirror. Whenever I didn't get the results I was looking for, instead of trying to pin the blame somewhere else, I would ask myself what I could have done better to get the job done. And 80 percent of the time, it hit me that I could have articulated the mission better, or provided better training, or given people more time and resources.

On the day I visited Brian's Huddle, someone brought up a problem at the call center. "When you try to book a job for an existing customer," she said, "the computer only allows you to treat it as though it's for a new customer, so a duplicate account is created, and that is causing a lot of problems." The leader of the Huddle thanked her for raising the issue, and appointed two call-center employees to be SPA for a solution.

Each day's Huddle is limited to ten minutes, but it's remarkable how much is accomplished in that brief period. Brian attributes the meeting's efficiency to the face-to-face interaction. "I've noticed as our company grows," he said, "that hiring more people doesn't always fix problems, because more people often means more distorted, diluted communication and less accountability. The Huddle lets all of us get together every day, the way a family does, so we're all on the same page."

Michael Bleier is a fan of huddles, too, and he's definitely onboard with the notion of not laying problems at the feet of any one person or team. At Able Distributors, the family-owned company he serves as vice president, huddles are used to advance the pursuit of a common goal: superior profitability. The huddles take place at weekly open-book management sessions in which the company's books are literally opened for viewing by all employees. People are then assigned responsibility for specific lines on the P&L statements for their own departments. The huddle thus brings people together as a team and reinforces the importance each player's assigned role has in reaching the common goal.

John Wade, when he was our combat systems officer, had huddles every day. They were extraordinarily productive, and I admired the way he ran them and how his people responded.

LEADERSHIP TRAINING PAYS DIVIDENDS.

The 1-800-GOT-JUNK? Huddle has also become a development tool. Traditionally, Brian has run the ten-minute meeting; not long ago, though, he asked himself why. "If we want to teach people how to be leaders and grow with the company," he told his top aides, "let's get them running the Huddle." So he sent an e-mail to everyone at headquarters announcing training for "Huddle masters" and asking for volunteers. Thirteen people signed on.

"I sat down with them," Brian recalled, "and I asked them why they thought we do Huddle, to make sure they were aligned with its goals. Then I asked how they would do Huddle differently." The volunteers came up with lots of ideas: People need to speak up, because sometimes Huddle is too noisy and you can't hear; people should stand closer to the leader; side conversations should not be allowed. Brian applauded their suggestions and said they should feel free to offer them when their turn came to run the Huddle.

One of the first new Huddle masters began by taping out a semicircle and asking everyone to move in close to the line so they could be more involved in the process. People hesitated, but then came forward. They have crowded the tape ever since. After that Huddle was over, this same first-time master pulled aside several frontline people and asked for a critique: What had he done well? What needed improving? That debriefing, too, became a tradition.

As a result of Brian's single training session, the volunteers took on responsibility for improving the Huddle. Meanwhile, their own work showed a sudden and marked improvement. One manager asked Brian, "What did you do in that training thing? Because whatever you did, it's had a big impact on those people—like, massive."

But, as Brian points out, "I didn't train them to do anything. I just got them to tell me what they thought we did well, what needed improving, and then allowed them to do it." That same willingness to "let them do it" unifies his staff and lifts morale.

Out in Oregon, Steve Smith has developed a similar unifying

technique for the employees of his Tec Labs: A half a day long, monthly gathering known as the Bagel Meeting, where employees can discuss work flow, bottlenecks, and planned expenditures. At least an hour is devoted to expressions of mutual accommodation and appreciation. "Everyone comes with something to say to someone. It could be as simple as saving the company twenty-five dollars on a shipping invoice, or special appreciation to the thoughtful gesture made by a coworker," Steve explained.

FACE-SAVING SOLUTIONS KEEP CREWS SMILING.

A big part of keeping a crew unified and working happily together is nothing more than old-fashioned mentoring, says Master Chief Bob Scheeler: "It's taking a chief by the hand, off to one side, and telling him that his behavior is this, or that his people are doing that." The quiet, one-on-one approach keeps people from losing face.

"Sometimes, our egos are so attached to certain things," Scheeler explains, "that the issue we're trying to deal with takes a backseat to being right or not losing face. No one wants to be publicly put in a position or made to feel that they were wrong," especially those in leadership roles. "You have to support those people who are supporting you," he advises. Sometimes, that means working a face-saving compromise. When there is a broken relationship between a chief and a division officer or a chief and a department head, for instance, the master chief has to intervene in a manner that keeps both parties from being embarrassed or deflated. People make mistakes and everyone knows it, but what the crew expects from its leaders is to be supported and directed toward the correct path in a positive way.

I could always count on Master Chief Scheeler to handle some of our toughest people issues in a very nonconfrontational, non-adversarial manner. Scheeler had an office, but he was never in it. I'd often see him topside with a young division officer, providing guidance in his disarming way.

HAND OUT MEDALS WHENEVER YOU CAN.

In the Navy, I found that praise was one of my most powerful motivators and unifying tools. So, in addition to writing letters of appreciation to the parents of young *Benfold* crew members when they achieved some measure of success, I also walked the ship daily and thanked my sailors in person. The more I thanked them, the harder they worked. I handed out 115 Navy Achievement Medals in my first year as commanding officer, instead of the fifteen authorized for my ship. And whenever a sailor left the ship, I made a short speech about his or her prized traits, while other shipmates often contributed accolades or funny stories. The effect was to reinforce the general feeling that the crew was a family.

In similar fashion, Steve Smith celebrates his employees' work anniversaries with a "living eulogy" delivered during a Bagel Meeting. Employees take turns speaking about the honoree in a way that's ordinarily reserved for fond remembrances at a wake or funeral. "The impact is profound," Steve said. "The person just sits there, hearing about all the things they are and all the things they've accomplished. There's a lot of tears. But it allows people to know that they're loved and cared for." Remember, Steve added, "the two big motivators in people's lives are love and respect."

STEER THE COCKIEST SAILORS INTO LEADERSHIP ROLES.

Benfold was equipped with the incredibly complex Aegis-missile fire-control system. Aegis-equipped vessels don't rely on separate radar systems for searching, tracking targets, and fire control. Instead, the system wraps the ship in a radar bubble that picks up a hostile intruder coming from any direction and shoots it down—all automatically and within a few seconds. The system costs hundreds of millions of dollars and the whole ship is built around it.

Not surprisingly, it takes a lot of brains to understand, operate, and repair such a sophisticated system, and the fire controlmen are the smartest sailors on the ship. They're identified through testing, school grades, and so forth, and then have to undergo a rigorous eighteen to twenty-four months of schooling to secure their jobs.

And because there's a market for these guys on the outside, the Navy gives them big retention bonuses to re-up. It all adds up to a penchant for arrogance—"Aegis arrogance," it's called—and the fire controlmen's attitude, coupled with their tendency to segregate themselves from the rest of the crew, became a source of resentment and discord on *Benfold*. The challenge was to bring these guys down a peg and back in line with the rest of the crew, but without humiliating them.

So when I had lunch on the mess decks on Wednesdays, I made

it a point to search out the fire controlmen, particularly Michael Pickett. He was an incredibly intelligent, incredibly talented technician who had what I thought was an incredibly annoying mouth that was never silent. Pickett personified the fire controlmen's arrogance that so infuriated the rest of the crew. He had an opinion about everything, and, to hear him tell it, he was always right—even about things that he knew little about, like how the ship should be run.

Now Pickett definitely knew more about the Aegis system than I could ever hope to, but his training and rating as a second-class petty officer certainly didn't qualify him to dictate how I should run our ship. So I used those Wednesday lunches to disabuse him of some really lousy ideas, correcting him in front of his tablemates and letting him know that he was not infallible. He started running his mouth a little less.

When I began to see that my criticism was sinking in, I then took Pickett aside and told him that, as the smartest guy on the ship, he could be a source of discontent and dissension or a source for good. Happily, Michael stepped up to the plate and assumed responsibility, becoming a true leader in every sense of the word. Having once been a malcontent himself, he became something of a spokesperson for the ship's other dissatisfied crew members. But, interestingly enough, with Michael as their spokesperson, the malcontents began to be less discontented.

SET HIGH STANDARDS.

Love and respect are like self-esteem: hollow if they're not earned. On *Benfold*, I tried in large part to unify the crew by insisting on high performance and a continual learning process. The Navy has a special program, the enlisted surface warfare specialist program (ESWS), designed to train sailors to go beyond their specialties and learn how their entire ship works. This training makes it easier to learn to backstop others, and it strengthens the ship's performance, especially in a crisis. Sailors who complete ESWS wear a special pin and earn bonus points toward promotion. But the program is so difficult that only the most experienced sailors usually sign up for it. And since hardly anyone had passed ESWS in my predecessor's time, the crew was convinced that it wasn't feasible.

So I streamlined the program, cutting out all the parts that didn't apply to *Benfold*—perhaps 15 percent of the total. Then I told the crew that learning ESWS would train them to show visitors around the ship, a duty that was becoming enormously popular. In that light, the program didn't look so hard, and nearly every sailor aboard signed up. In short order, we qualified nearly 200 of our 310 crew members.

One of the qualifiers was Sarah Garner, the combat fire control technician who was shocked to learn that disgruntled crew members on my predecessor's watch hid themselves away to avoid duty. Sarah became a great success, eventually getting selected for chief petty officer in eight years instead of the usual fourteen, and she was always one of the first to take on new jobs and learn entire new systems.

At the beginning, the ESWS program looked impossible, she told me recently, "but it ended up being fun. What it did was, it got you out talking to everyone. You got a chance to interact with other people on the ship whose jobs were so dissimilar from yours that you might not have a lot of interaction with them otherwise." One day, on a missile training exercise with two other ships, Sarah found herself at a watch station in the combat systems co-ordinator's office, where she realized that, on the other ships, the corresponding stations were being manned by a lieutenant and a master chief. At that point, she was still a second-class petty officer. Both of us were proud of what she had achieved.

In civilian life, Sarah has used her talent for learning to boot-strap herself to a unique position. As the special projects coor-dinator for an entrepreneur who owns seventeen companies in Pennsylvania, she moves from one business to another to take on whatever project requires the boss's personal representative. She's a walking demonstration of what the Navy can do for its enlisted people. And every day, she applies the lessons she learned on *Ben-fold*—in particular, that an organization is far more effective if its people understand each other's jobs and why things are done.

Early in her business life, when she was selling health insur-ance, she asked the customer-service supervisor how she wanted the paperwork done—a question that the astonished supervisor had never been asked before. Sarah had figured out that if she gave her supervisor the paperwork the way she needed it, "My paperwork would get through faster and my clients would get enrolled faster. It really worked well for me," Sarah said. By the same token, she learned enough about underwriting to know what benefits she could promise her clients without fear that their applications would be turned down. You might think that ought to be standard practice, and it probably should be, but no one did it until Sarah came along.

Sarah put herself in the shoes of her customers and the people she was trying to influence. On *Benfold*, we always tried to put ourselves in the shoes of our boss—the admiral—and anticipate his needs before he knew what they were. Then we put the processes in place ahead of time so that when he determined what he needed, he would also know that *Benfold* would come through. That's how you become the go-to ship. That's also how you become the go-to person and how you make people trust you—the subject of the next chapter.

CHAPTER 5

FOUL WEATHER DOESN'T RESPECT RANK

CREATING A CLIMATE OF TRUST

IN THE NAVY AS IN BUSINESS, IT TAKES MORE THAN A SIMPLE order to keep your crew functioning smoothly. The whole organization has to have an atmosphere that encourages people to trust one another.

Creating a climate of trust starts with the captain. If the sailors see him as devious, self-serving, inconsistent, or hypocritical, they will instinctively distrust him. Prior to my arrival, the sailors on *Benfold* saw themselves as pawns in the captain's schemes to get promoted; they felt they were constantly made to do chores that made the captain look good but added nothing to the ship's performance. Whether it's true or not, that's how they viewed themselves, and it was demoralizing for them. Whenever a dignitary was coming aboard, the sailors had to paint the ship—not necessarily because it needed paint, but just to make it look nice. Sometimes the paint was still wet when the guest arrived, and the captain's tour would leave two sets of footprints visible all around the deck. The sailors groused that the captain was using their lips to kiss the admiral's ass.

In a climate like that, distrust runs rampant. And since the captain's behavior sets the tone for the whole ship, the officers relaying and carrying out his commands will be seen as equally devious, manipulative, and self-serving. Soon, most of the crew will learn to "go along to get along," transparently working to promote themselves instead of the ship and its mission. Cynicism will become universal, and the sailors' distrust will spread to include all but their closest friends onboard.

In tense situations, people get nervous and worried that others don't appreciate what they are doing. I've seen distrust spread like wildfire. In fact, it singed me soon after I boarded USS *Harry W. Hill* as the new combat systems officer. *Hill* was a relatively new destroyer, one of the most advanced warships in the Pacific Fleet at the time. I was a first-time department head, suddenly charged with guiding an electronic marvel in combat situations. Talk about tension.

My previous tour on the rust bucket *Albert David* had taught me zip about my new job. I was not even remotely prepared to stand watch in the combat information center as the tactical action officer (TAO). *Harry W. Hill* had three department heads and because of our seniority, we stood the TAO duties 24/7 while at sea, spending six hours on watch and twelve hours off.

I found myself struggling to carry out my TAO duties on *Harry W. Hill* in my first full-scale war exercise with the battle group.

We were screening the aircraft carrier USS *Carl Vinson*, named for a congressman famously kind to Navy budgets, and we were charged with defending the *Vinson* from a submarine attack. My job was to coordinate a complex listening process that required aircraft to drop sound-detection devices at exactly the right ocean spot and depth for locating "enemy" submarines and "sinking" them before they torpedoed the carrier.

Sorry to say, I did such a poor job that, three days into the exercise, my executive officer, Lieutenant Commander Dave Ryan, called me the worst TAO he'd ever seen. I couldn't disagree. In a real war, I'm not sure Carl Vinson himself could have survived even one day of my submarine tech work, capped by fatal mis-triangulations.

Fortunately, this was a training exercise, so I had time to improve, at least a bit. But, unfortunately, there came a time, later in the exercise, when the submarines were tracking surface ships, including us. To help confuse them, we all turned off our radars so that the submarines could not pick us out from our electromagnetic emissions. However, no radar also meant we were unable to judge the distance of other surface objects on a very dark moonless night. Without radar, there was essentially nothing for us to do in the combat information center, so I chose to get caught up on paperwork, something there's never a shortage of.

At the same time, the OOD (officer of the deck) spotted the running lights of another ship in the darkness. He directed the signalman to use a flashing light to request its ID in Morse code. The signalman said it was the USS *Vincennes*, one of our fellow cruisers. Seeing no need to change course, the OOD steamed ahead. I heard all of this on the intercom and thought that the OOD—who is responsible for the safety of navigation and for adhering to the rules of the nautical road—had everything under control.

Suddenly, I felt *Harry W. Hill* lunging hard-right rudder. The signalman was wrong. The other ship was the enormous carrier *Carl Vinson*, bearing down on us at full speed with the right of way. We missed a serious collision by the skin of our teeth. And nothing ends Navy careers faster than collisions at sea. Courts-martial are mandatory.

I had nothing whatever to do with the near-miss. But because my TAO mishaps had quickly cast a dark cloud of distrust over me, I became the scapegoat for the incident. The captain was visibly shaken and disappointed in me. David Ryan, the XO, reamed me out at length. I was minutes away from being fired.

Here's what I learned from this incident: Distrust can sink ships and careers, so build trust at all costs.

Accordingly, I set about fervently trying to build my own trustworthiness aboard *Harry W. Hill*. I did it by working around the clock to master the mysteries of being a good TAO and running the combat information center to near perfection. It wasn't easy for me. But because it was my major weakness, I gave it everything I had. Some people advise you to forget about your weaknesses and focus only on improving your strengths. That sounds good in theory, but I clearly would have been fired had I not improved. When I left *Harry W. Hill* eighteen months later, David Ryan told me I was the best TAO he had ever seen.

Command is a lonely thing, we are often told, and only one person fills the captain's shoes. Such clichés are true, but they tend to be used to justify skippers who fit the classic authoritarian mold. The truly successful captain also has the special gift to coax ordinary people to do amazing things. The average sailor or officer will not toil, much less die, for a distant boss enfolded in his own mystique. The leader we leap to work for is neither a buddy nor a father figure; instead, he is a caring, brave, honest straight-shooter with great skills, an indelible presence, and a humble, easy manner with his people that never endangers his necessary distance. Above all, we trust him—trust him to look out for us while bringing out our best in the job we all share.

This chapter describes the efforts that my crew and I devoted to that relationship on *Benfold*—efforts that will surely work for you as well as they did for us.

PUT YOUR CREW'S INTERESTS FIRST.

I couldn't order *Benfold*'s crew to trust me, and it took a while before they did. But I can pinpoint the day the climate started to change. It was two months after I had taken command. We were en route to the Middle East with *Harry W. Hill* and *Gary*. The commodore was embarked on *Hill*. We were doing an exercise near Pearl Harbor that was supposed to end at five on a Friday afternoon, when we would pull into port for liberty. When Navy ships enter port, they line up according to the rank of the senior officers onboard. Therefore, *Harry W. Hill* and the commodore were to lead the way. The captain on *Gary* was senior to me, so we would go in last.

Instead of finishing at 5:00 p.m., we were done at 8 a.m. But we didn't head to port. The ships were just sitting out there, cutting holes in the ocean. I was looking through my binoculars at Waikiki, thinking how great it would be to drink a mai-tai on the beach. I called the captain of *Harry W. Hill*, recommending that he ask the commodore for permission to go in early; he told me he had an engineering problem that could only be fixed at sea, so we would all stay out. I called *Gary*'s captain, who admonished me on the radio to stick to the plan and not challenge authority. That's when I called the commodore directly, using the radio that any sailor on any ship could monitor.

When the commodore answered, I realized he had been listening to my previous calls and was not in a good mood. He wasted no time demanding to know why I thought *Benfold* should be granted a favor that other ships didn't get. I explained that the exercise had ended well before schedule, and that by steaming all day waiting for the other ships, we would be burning fuel, wasting taxpayers' money. Besides, I had a broken piece of equipment that needed fixing. Most important, though, I wanted to put my sailors on the beach.

Much to my surprise, the commodore cleared his throat and said, "Permission granted." Most of my sailors were assembled in the combat information center, two decks below my cabin, and I could hear them cheering through two decks of steel. With permission granted, I put all four engines in gear and steamed into port at full speed, shooting a two-story-high rooster tail off the fantail. We normally steam around on one engine, and you can do up to eighteen knots on that engine. You can do twenty-four knots on two engines, twenty-seven knots on three, and thirty-one-plus on four engines. But you can use four times as much gas. We saved not one drop of gas, but my sailors were enjoying the Hawaiian sun and waves by one o'clock that afternoon.

The next day, heading for Singapore, Petty Officer Jeremy Zeller came in for one of my crew interviews. He said, "You know, Captain, it seems to us like you don't care if you ever get promoted again." I asked, "What on earth gave you that idea?" He smiled and said, "What you did yesterday . . . you had nothing to gain from it. We know you did it for us, and we want you to know we're never going to let you down."

That was the day I knew I had earned the trust of my crew by showing them that I put their needs ahead of my own.

A CLIMATE OF TRUST HINGES ON MORE THAN PEOPLE; SYSTEMS MUST BE NURTURED, TOO.

It takes a lot of energy to deep-six a long-standing climate of distrust, and once you've earned your crew's (or your customers') trust, it takes a constant effort to keep it. But earn it you must. For as Michael Bleier is quick to point out, "Trust is earned, not given."

Michael had been a part of his family's wholesale heating and cooling business for over twelve years when he came to the conclusion that the company was floating along on a tide of mediocrity. And for it to become the superior business he knew it could be, the workforce had to be inspired to perform at its highest level, which could only happen if they trusted their leaders to look out for their best interests and took pride in what their company was trying to achieve.

So Able Distributors, at Michael's prodding, convinced its employees of the rightness of its aim to sell the best products, offer the best service, and earn the highest profits, all the while assuring them that while everything was possible, none of it could be accomplished without their help. So with a lot of reassurance, a lot of communication, and a lot of humility from the leaders, the trust began to build.

But despite the workforce's growing trust in its bosses and their motives, the staff was not entirely won over. Why? Because they were forced to rely on undependable systems, particularly the computer system. "If the computer said we had four of something," Michael told me, "there was probably a 90 percent chance that we didn't have four. We might have two or twenty, but we definitely didn't have four." How could a conscientious employee be expected to deal happily and efficiently with a contractor calling on the phone to ask for, say, four couplings? "The computer says four but I don't think so," was a typical response. "Let me go check."

Now, it doesn't take an efficiency expert to see that an ingrained mistrust of the computer system was costing Able time and money and the patience of its customers, who no doubt found it extremely annoying to waste their time on the phone while a well-meaning employee searched the warehouse for requested parts. Surely, customers themselves will eventually lose trust in a company whose employees can't seem to trust the systems and equipment their company has provided for them.

Ships in the Navy have to carry spare parts as well, and it was always maddening when the computer said we had ten widgets onboard but they didn't seem to be in the supply bins when we needed them. Nothing was more demotivating, both to the storekeepers and the technicians who needed the spare parts to keep their equipment running.

One of Dave Devlin's first tasks when he took over as supply officer was to beef up the computer system so that it accurately reflected what was in the storage bins. It wasn't sexy or glamorous work, but the supply chain never is. Yet, as we all know, it doesn't matter how brilliant your business plan is; if you don't have the materials you need when you need them, you're in trouble. If dedicated and motivated people don't execute their jobs flawlessly, the trains don't run on time. On many occasions, the differentiator between you and your competitors is which of you executes the simple things extraordinarily well. That's all done with people.

IF YOU DON'T CARE, THEY WON'T TRUST.

Long after my Navy career was over, I saw the distrust syndrome at work behind the Hertz Gold counter at a major midwestern airport. It was early in the evening in February, with a twenty-mile-per-hour wind whipping outside and the temperature at two below zero. Hertz promises to expedite the rental process for gold card members; your name goes up on a board and you go straight to the stall where your car is parked.

But on this night, the board wasn't working, and perhaps forty of Hertz's best customers were standing in a line that stretched out into the cold as they waited for the one young woman behind the counter to tell them where to find their cars. I asked her if the manager knew that all these "best customers" were waiting, and she said, in front of everyone, "The manager doesn't care." Along the line of customers, jaws dropped.

So I walked behind the counter and opened the door to the backroom, and there sat the manager with seven other workers. I said, "You know, you've got forty people waiting in line out there. I thought you might want to know since it's so cold outside." He said he knew. Four minutes later, one person came out to help. That's what happens when one bad leader poisons the atmosphere, betrays the trust, and sabotages the whole operation.

Especially in the military's traditional command-and-control climate, it's tempting for an officer to believe that his rank signifies that he is superior in every way—smarter, better informed, more talented, and, in general, a higher class of being than anyone ranked lower. Common sense contradicts such a lofty view; obviously, the captain gets just as wet in a storm as any sailor, and both of them will drown if the ship goes down. If the captain can drop his God-like attitude and learn to respect his sailors' real talents and special qualities, they will come to trust him and work a lot harder than they ever will for a self-important fool.

PURSUE EXCELLENCE WITHOUT ARROGANCE.

I've spent a lot of time these past few years reflecting on why William Perry became such a wonderful role model—for me and for countless others whose lives he has touched. What was so appealing, I think, was his humility. Perry was a very self-effacing leader. People were drawn to him, and his modesty made the jobs of military people easier around the globe. It meant something to go to a foreign country and find, thanks to him, that we were respected.

In comparison, Secretary of Defense Donald Rumsfeld made our jobs more difficult around the world, both during his tenure and now. Rumsfeld is obviously a brilliant man, but his seemingly arrogant style turns people off. In business, too, it is far better to lead with modesty rather than arrogance, because when times get tough, people will stick with the leaders they are attracted to and respect. Charles R. Larson, who retired as superintendent of the Naval Academy in 1998, summed it up when he told the midshipmen they needed to create a sense of excellence without arrogance. And to me, that's the ticket to creating something sustainable for the long term.

NEVER PULL RANK.

A good leader treats his people with courtesy and respect, whatever their rank. A martinet who thinks those on the rungs below are a lower order of being will be obeyed, but he will never inspire his crew to do their best. In any case, pulling rank isn't in anyone's self-interest. Life is a marathon, not a sprint. If you step on people on your way up the ladder, no one will stick out a hand when you fall.

A captain I'll call John found that out the hard way. He was the commanding officer of a cruiser and was one of the most senior captains in the Pacific. I was aboard his ship as aide to Admiral Hugh Webster, a two-star. John seemed to look down his nose at all the captains who were junior to him, including another of the admiral's staff, Dave McKinley.

One Sunday morning after church in Subic Bay, John walked up to McKinley, jabbed his finger in his chest, and told him, without any provocation, "You're a disgrace to the U.S. Navy." McKinley was nothing of the sort. He was a gentleman, and he never pushed back. Even though his wife was beside him when he was insulted, he held his tongue out of respect for John's seniority.

Just two months later, John ran his cruiser aground. The damage was going to cost about $10 million to repair, and the four-star admiral of the Pacific Fleet ordered Admiral Webster to investigate the cause. The admiral took me and Dave McKinley to conduct the inquiry.

John didn't seem bothered by Webster coming aboard, but when he saw McKinley, he visibly blanched. In that moment, I'm sure many things went through his mind, one of which was a wish that he had treated McKinley better. I'm equally sure that Dave wasn't a vindictive man. But after our report, John was relieved for cause. Thirty sailors had known that his cruiser was about to run aground. Because of his penchant for shooting bad-news messengers, everyone was afraid to tell him the truth. Your seniority matters not when you've run aground.

ALWAYS GO THE EXTRA NAUTICAL MILE.

I was never more disheartened in a ship's command than at the end of our 100 days in the Persian Gulf. *Benfold* had been the workhorse the whole time, doing everything asked of us and more. The crew knew we'd been working harder than any other ship. The sailors on *Harry W. Hill*, for instance, had spent most of their 100 days sitting next to the pier, unable to carry out their missions, while *Benfold* took on their assignments in addition to our own. And now, as we were preparing to head to Australia for twelve days of port visits, Commodore Mike Duffy tasked us with one last mission. He was out of assets, there was a smuggler, and he needed a ship to track it. So he got on the secure satellite radio and asked us to do it.

I looked around, seeing the hopeful faces of my crew, willing me to say no. Much to the crew's dismay, I said, "Commodore, we're your ship." Everyone, including me, was absolutely heartbroken that we'd be losing some of our port visits. But for three days, we tracked the smuggler while the other ships steamed toward Australia.

Finally, the commodore found another ship to take over the job, and relieved us. Later, Duffy called me on the radio and said, "How much extra fuel would you need to catch up to the other ships?" Off the top of my head, I said it would mean doubling our fuel allotment, a supply I didn't think he had. But Duffy said, "You got it. Catch up to the other ships, and you won't miss a day in Australia."

I hadn't expected to be rewarded. I just knew that when something had to be done, *Benfold* should be the first ship everyone thought of. Commodore Duffy knew he could trust us to go the extra mile and took care of us in return. Being on the go-to team can be hard, but it always pays off in the long run.

TRUST, TRAIN, AND DELEGATE.

Though I didn't intend it as a way to promote a climate of trust, my system of delegating authority turned out to do just that. The need for a new system was obvious. In my first years in the Navy, the technology was so rudimentary that a ship was able to concentrate on only one mission at a time. *Albert David* could do any of four tasks, but not more than one of them at once. If we were hunting submarines, no one expected us to bombard the shore or look for aircraft or missiles at the same time. The captain could give his whole attention to the job at hand, and he was in charge.

But by the time I took over *Benfold*, technology was developing at Internet speed and had become so integrated that we were expected to handle all six of our capabilities at once—and do it with 35 percent fewer sailors than *Albert David* had had twenty years before. I could have micromanaged one or two areas, but the others would have fallen apart. The only way I could run six warfare areas simultaneously was by training subordinates and delegating responsibility, with backups trained to handle every job on the ship. So I put senior people in charge of each mission area, bringing me in on decisions only when necessary. For instance, if a situation got to the point where we had to fire a gun, I was the only one who could give final approval. But up to that point, I needed to know only when things went wrong or if one of my trip wires was hit.

Because I trusted my people to handle so much authority, they learned to trust one another, too, and it spread throughout the crew. Sailors were loyal to their petty officers because they wanted to make them look good so that the whole unit would get more credit.

Bill Walsh used this same tactic in coaching the 49ers—and it worked. Knowing his players wanted to protect their assistant coaches, he would criticize the coach rather than the player for a misplay. It was hard on the coaches, but the players were more motivated by their desire to make their coaches look good than they would have been by a direct rebuke.

DON'T OVERLOOK THE SAILORS IN
BLUE SHIRTS.

On *Benfold*, the training of backups helped strengthen the climate of trust. Backups are always needed, if only because you never know when someone will get sick or injured or suddenly be transferred to another ship. But if you get into combat, you also have to worry about replacing casualties. So I wanted to have four people trained to handle every critical job on the ship, and that meant reaching down several layers to man some positions. For example, I needed my senior officers to be in the combat information center to handle those six mission areas, which forced me to break the tradition that only officers can stand watch as officer of the deck.

The officer of the deck drives the ship at sea, giving orders to the helmsman and the engine room. In fact, everyone on the bridge team works for him, including ensigns and junior lieutenants. It's an important job, and the safety of the ship depends on doing it right. The hierarchy of command has traditionally ruled out giving the job to anyone but an officer. But because I needed my officers below, I allowed a petty officer, First Class Signalman Michael Murray, to drive the ship. He had shown quickness and intelligence as a signaler, and I told him, "Even though you're an E-6 and a blue shirt, I'd make you officer of the deck if you want it."

Michael trained hard, got selected for officer of the deck, and became one of the best on *Benfold*. He had a seaman's eye and a tremendous gift for driving a ship, and he went on to a special program to become an officer. His success was a powerful sign that talent was where we found it, and hard work would be rewarded, but it was also a lesson in trust. For if the captain would trust a petty officer to drive the ship, the rest of the sailors knew they could step up for any job they were fit for and would trust that their merits would be recognized.

Michael Murray's rise became one of the stories *Benfold* sailors bragged about on shore leave when they met people from other ships. Another was about a submarine-hunting exercise that I turned into a case study in building trust.

We were on the way to Hawaii and had already done this exercise twice, following the standard Navy approach—a model that had been received wisdom ever since World War II. Needless to say, everyone was a little bored with it. So, after asking the squadron commander for permission to lead this time, I told John Wade, the weapons department head, to come up with a new plan. But I didn't want John to do it himself; I wanted the enlisted men, the radar operators, technicians, and gunners to work up the plan.

John told me later how hard it was to stand back and let the sailors run the show, but he did, and some twenty excited, revved-up sailors came up with a unique sub-hunting strategy. It didn't work. John was very upset. It was his group's plan, so he felt like a failure. And, as he told me later, he couldn't understand why I was smiling and patting people on the back.

After the exercise, we did a "hot wash-up," a public discussion of the outcome, with all participating ships listening in. I got on the radio and thanked the commodore for letting us run the exercise. I said I had asked my team to come up with an innovative plan to see if it would work, and obviously it hadn't. However, I added, this was one of the proudest moments of my command. My junior sailors were better for having immersed themselves in tactics and for learning what works and what doesn't. *Benfold* was a better ship, too, I said.

Then I put down the mike and spoke to my people directly, telling them they had made me proud. Their chests were puffed out, too, because I had trusted them enough to try their plan at the risk of looking foolish if it failed. And when their plan didn't work, I didn't hold it against them. Their trust in me was greater than ever, and all of us were certain that we'd do better next time.

We learn from our failures. To me, standing in the box and swinging away is what we're here for. But my beliefs and instincts went against the grain of the Navy I was serving. In the 1990s, the brass hats were looking for excuses to get rid of people and not promote them. This led to a "zero-defect" mentality; even one black mark on your record because you tried something and failed got you drummed out of the military. It was a culture of risk aversion, and people stopped trying things because of their fear of failing.

Business, of course, isn't immune to this ailment. In 2002, I was asked to speak to an automotive finance company. The two guys who hired me, Scott Cochran and Rob Glander, took me aside to say that the problem with their company was that too many people were hiding. I had to laugh, remembering Sarah Garner telling me about the hiding places on *Benfold* before I arrived.

Since leaving the Navy, I've seen lots of people hiding in plain sight. They don't want to push the envelope, try new things, and improve their companies. They're just answering the mail, hoping nothing bad happens before they reach retirement age. I tried to make my sub-hunting crew feel in their bones that they had pushed the envelope, that they were out and about trying new things. I and my crew might not be perfect, but at least we were constantly pushing, and improvement was sure to follow.

BE FRIENDLY, BUT DON'T BE A FRIEND.

To win trust, a leader must be approachable and show a genuine interest in what his people think and do. On *Benfold*, I made it a point to make regular rounds of the whole ship, hobnobbing with everyone I met. I also ate at least one meal each week with the crew on the mess deck, usually the cheeseburger lunch on Wednesdays. It was a chance to shoot the breeze with my sailors, listen to their concerns, and show once again that we were all on the same side, working toward the same goals.

There's a fine line to be drawn here. There are captains who suck up to their crews, trying so hard to be democratic and easygoing that they undermine discipline, end-run their officers, and ultimately lose all respect. I took pains always to be the captain, with all the authority the position merits, and I never got overly chummy or encouraged disparaging talk about my officers. But within those bounds, I tried to be approachable, affable, and always interested in anything my sailors wanted to tell me.

Teresa White at Aflac also believes in getting close to her employees, but closeness stops short of personal friendship. "I let them know that business is business," she told me. "I expect results. But I make sure that people know I will always respect them and their opinions, even if I don't always do things their way." And Teresa has developed what may be a unique way to stay accessible and open the lines of communication. "I periodically hijack meetings," she told me rather gleefully. She drops in on team sessions unannounced, catches up on progress, and then gives people a chance to ask her questions. Particularly for newcomers to Aflac, these unexpected and casual visits demonstrate how approachable their leader really is.

At 1-800-GOT-JUNK?, Brian Scudamore takes a similar approach. Rather than lock himself away behind closed doors or bury himself in paperwork, Brian looks around the office, watches the goings-on, and listens to the conversations. Watching, listening, and asking questions are his way of taking the company's pulse. As Brian described it to me, amid the office's purposeful bustle, "I'm just kicked back, not relaxed exactly, but sort of like standing on the tallest tree in the forest, watching, listening, maybe asking some questions."

Like me, Brian has made himself the visible fabric of his organization. People aren't surprised to see him, and they don't shut up when he comes around. I tried to set the same tone on *Benfold*. My door was always open, and people knew they could come in if they wanted. Or I might go down and sit in the engineering central control station, just listening while the engineers came and went as they kept the ship steaming along. By becoming part of the routine, I got to see things the way they actually were, instead of seeing only what my crew might have wanted me to see.

Truly entrepreneurial leaders—those preparing themselves for the future—make a point of being among their people, not above them. James H. Patterson, cofounder of National Cash Register (NCR), was a pioneer of worker-friendly leadership. In the 1890s, he located his office on the factory floor in Dayton, Ohio. Positioned for hands-on analyses of working conditions, he soon launched then unheard-of improvements: clean work areas, dressing rooms with lockers and showers, hot lunches, movies, health clinics, night classes, regular vacations. NCR factories, once dark and gloomy, were redesigned as "daylight factories" with four-fifths of the walls made of glass. Patterson was a one-man precursor of human-resource departments, but bureaucracies would not have pleased him. His boss concept was all about respecting worker dignity.

A more contemporary example is New York's Mayor Michael Bloomberg. While building his financial information business, he didn't hide away in a corner office with river views. He sat in the center of the newsroom as the company's business whirred around him. People realized that he didn't set himself apart from anyone else. Like other outstanding grassroots leaders, Bloomberg defined his culture by being a part of it.

So did Paul O'Neill, the former CEO of Alcoa and the Bush administration's first treasury secretary. At Alcoa, O'Neill sat surrounded by all his executives, enjoying an open, free exchange of ideas.

Brian Scudamore hobnobs with his people in various ways. Sometimes, he motions for people to come to his desk for a chat. More often, he turns an unscheduled encounter in the hallway or office into an occasion for listening. He asks workers at every level of the company how their day is going, and he actually waits for a complete answer.

Like my lunches on the mess deck, Brian has his own tradition, known as the CEO lunch. Every week, he takes two or three staffers from different parts of the company out for food and some frank, confidential talk about what's right and wrong at 1-800-GOT-JUNK?, and what can be done to improve things. "My role is to get out there and say, 'Hey, want to go grab a coffee? Let's walk down the street to Starbucks.' Or if I see someone I haven't spent time with recently, I take him or her to lunch. I find that I learn so much more, and really absorb a lot more of value, by doing so."

DISPENSE DISCIPLINE WITH AN EVEN HAND.

Master Chief Bob Scheeler knows a thing or two about earning trust. As the direct representative of the crew to me, he had a lot of people who looked to him for help and guidance. And one of the thorniest problems we faced together was having to discipline one of his chief petty officers, who just happened to be a woman.

As the first combat ship in the Navy that was built from the keel up for a mixed-gendered crew and with a mixed-gendered philosophy in mind, *Benfold* was destined to be a unique experience from Day One. And this situation proved the point. At the time, women were relatively new to serving on combat ships, and a lot of adapting had to be done on the fly.

Knowing that this woman would be filling the position in the division that he himself had been trained for, Scheeler made a conscious decision not to interfere with her job or undermine her ability to do what she was trained for. "I didn't want to run her division," he says, "and I wanted to make sure she clearly understood that it wasn't my role to run her division."

Friction developed, though, because she had a steep learning curve and didn't understand the mechanics of how combat ships work and how chief messes are supposed to work. "She didn't understand that I was the master chief but that we all still had a boss," Scheeler says. There was still a division officer to answer to and a department head.

She did a good job taking care of her people, the master chief says, but he worried that she sometimes failed to support the mission. "I'd have to take her aside on many occasions," he recalls, "and try to explain to her the big picture and how it works, and this is why we have to do the things we have to do."

It was a tricky situation from the start, since we desperately needed her to be successful. But the challenge got even bigger when she got romantically involved with one of the crew members, which is strictly forbidden.

Fraternization in the military is forbidden because it can create a hostile work environment and decrease combat readiness. Since women were so new to warships, there were a lot of very sensitive issues to be resolved. One of the trickiest was dating. Some of the old school said there would be no dating. Period. While this would have been a very neat and tidy policy, it was unworkable, unenforceable, and unrealistic. As we all know, when policies are unrealistic in the real world, people start defying them and pretty soon discipline breaks down.

We and the Navy eventually settled on what was probably the most enlightened solution possible. Dating was not permitted if there was a senior–subordinate relationship, officers could only date officers, chiefs could only date chiefs, and the crew could date if one of them did not have supervisory responsibility over the other. This way, no one could exert seniority to force a relationship.

The only recourse for me and the master chief was to take disciplinary action, and that was something that neither of us wanted to do. Yet, as Scheeler explains, "you never want to give the perception that things are going on with the chiefs and that the master chief is covering it up because it's one of them." To maintain the crew's trust, there was nothing to be done other than mete out proper punishment. "You had to be willing to dispense the discipline equally among your own," Scheeler says, just as you would among your subordinates.

Unfortunately, Scheeler and I had to take the woman to what's called the captain's mast. That's a non-judicial disciplinary hearing before a ship's commanding officer, originally conducted on deck at the main mast. Captains are authorized to impose penalties such as loss of pay, rank, or liberty ashore, the assignment of extra duties—and even to kick sailors out of the Navy.

Our female chief's mast was very painful but we had no choice. She had broken the rules and we had to do what we had to do, which was to send the message that, no matter who you are or what your job is, we all have to live by the rules and be held accountable.

Although this woman made a terrible mistake, she had become a good chief. And luckily for her, the command master chief and I both preached redemption. No matter what you had done, within reason, you could always overcome it and know that the sun will come out tomorrow. Or, as we liked to say, "The sun always shines on *Benfold*."

In fact, we had a very clever program that dated back to my predecessor, who, despite his seeming inability to connect with his crew, really hated to dole out punishment. No commanding officer likes to hold captain's mast. Because it has the potential to ruin careers, it is one of the most distasteful aspects of the job.

My predecessor's program made great use of a loophole in the rules, which I never knew existed. Essentially, he came up with a way for rule breakers to redeem themselves if they served their punishment, did their jobs correctly, and stayed out of trouble during the ninety-day review process after formal discipline was meted out. If they became model citizens, we would even expunge the offense from their record as if it had never happened.

Now Master Chief Scheeler will readily admit that, being from the old school, he was not in favor of giving second chances. But it was the previous captain's decision to make, telling Scheeler, as he recalls, "You know what, Command Master Chief? I am the captain and it's my ship, and this is the way we are going to play ball." The master chief answered, "Yes, sir," walked out the door, and carried on as if it was his own idea, telling the chief's mess how it was going to be. There was fierce resistance from the chiefs, but they had no say in the matter.

The funny thing was that Bob Scheeler himself approached me shortly after I came aboard to tell me about the ninety-day review policy for disciplinary cases and to urge me to keep it in place. At first I was resistant, too, since I had never seen it used before, and the Navy's disciplinary process was one program that I was wary of tinkering with. But he persuaded me, partly because I knew he was "old school" and even so favored this revolutionary idea. And we used it to allow the chief petty officer to redeem herself, with no damage done to her career.

For his part, Scheeler marvels that there was never a repeat offender after the review policy was instituted. "We never had a guy that we let him redeem himself who went back for a second trip," he says. I wonder if this redemption program could work in our criminal justice system?

PERFECTION ISN'T A PREREQUISITE.

You don't have to be a model leader to make these techniques work and win your people's trust. If you make an honest effort to build a relationship, they will cut you some slack even if you fumble once in a while.

I witnessed this reaction at one of the country's largest law firms, where the chief financial officer's operation had gotten a C-minus on the firm's annual employee satisfaction survey. The CFO wanted to do better. But when I spent a day with him, I saw that he lacked charisma, confidence, and presence. He wanted to be a great leader but had no idea how to go about it. I told him some of the things I did on *Benfold*, and he chose to try the tactics that felt comfortable to him, beginning with one-on-one interviews with his people.

A month later, one of the employees e-mailed me to say that she had worked twenty feet away from her boss for seven years, and he never knew her name. Now, he not only knew her name but after interviewing her and listening to her ideas, he had put some of them into practice. This employee suddenly felt she had a seat at the table. And getting to know her boss showed her that he wasn't a mean person, just shy and introverted; that's why he hadn't known her name.

This fellow has since interviewed every one of his employees, and his department now rates an A-plus in employee satisfaction. What's more, the entire law firm has adopted his methods, leading *Fortune* magazine to rank it as roughly the 150th best place to work in the United States.

This turnabout didn't occur because the CFO suddenly became a gung-ho leader; he'll never be that. But he has learned to be authentic, and that goes a long way with people. The interview process allowed him to transcend his introversion and reveal his underlying empathy, kindness, and unflappable competence. He has emerged as a genuine, down-to-earth person who, despite his shyness, cares for his people, and they are rewarding him with increased trust and performance.

You can do the same. Even if you're not a reincarnation of Mother Teresa with the flair of P. T. Barnum, you can learn to overcome your flaws and win your people's trust. And when they trust you, you can explain your organization's mission and clarify its goals in terms they will believe and understand. The next chapter tells you how.

CHAPTER 6

NAVIGATE BY THE STARS

CLARIFYING WHAT IT'S ALL ABOUT

FOR ANY LEADER WORKING TO GET THE WHOLE CREW ROW-ing in the same direction, it is crucial to make sure everyone understands the basic mission and the priorities you've set—for the long term, for the week, and for right now.

It's your job to communicate all this, to get feedback on whether the communication got through, to find out whether what you've ordered is working, and to be open to a better idea when it shows up. And it all has to be done in terms your people will understand.

Older generations typically complain about those coming along behind. But I've found that today's young people are no better or worse than any others. They do, however, have their own language, and it's up to the leader to communicate to them in their terms. I also tried to put myself in their world and view situations and life through their eyes. But be forewarned: It's a never-ending task, and you can't let up for a minute.

On *Benfold*, I used every opportunity I could find to get the word out and clear up confusion and misunderstandings. Nearly every one-on-one meeting with a member of the crew was a chance to pound home another piece of the message. I also used, among other tools, the public address system, the ship's newsletter, bulletin boards, and reminders posted in the corridors. I reinforced the message with my own behavior and tried to make sure my officers did the same.

At Philadelphia Insurance Companies, Jamie Maguire is intent on perpetuating the culture that he believes is necessary for his company's continued success. Maguire, the triathlete I introduced in Chapter 2, sees parallels between being able to compete in triathlons and in business. Both demand a dogged work ethic, dedication to a goal, an intense hunger to improve constantly, and a determination to succeed.

As a triathlete who came back from a devastating accident that broke his neck, jaw, hand, and kneecaps to reenter world-class competition while taking his company to new heights, Maguire models the characteristics and behaviors that he wants his workforce to emulate. The only way to teach your people, he says, is first to set an example and then reward those who pick up the cultural torch and carry it throughout the company. He rewards such employees with cash bonuses, items displaying the company logo, and a rewards program based on a point system.

Yet, it's not the cash and gifts that employees crave, Maguire says; it's the public acclaim. People like it when their fellow employees know they've done well and the company praises their accomplishments.

Like me strolling the decks of *Benfold* and talking to crew members, Maguire visits his employees around the country and holds quarterly town hall–type meetings so that he can get to know them and, more important, so they can come to know him and hear him describe the state of the company. Knowing the boss is a prerequisite for knowing the culture.

Maguire gives a lot of the credit for perpetuating the culture at Philadelphia Insurance to his old hands, people he refers to as "culture carriers." Even a superb communicator like Jamie Maguire can't shoulder the whole burden of building and preserving a company's culture, however. That's where longtime managers and executives who've internalized your culture can step up and keep the torch burning. But whether it's the captain or his chiefs who are preserving the ship's culture, it all comes down to one thing, says Maguire: communication. You must communicate honestly and often, in language that all of your diverse workforce can understand.

To give you an idea of the range of possibilities for communicating your message, I hung up a painting that served as one small part of this endless conversation with the crew. I used the picture to educate the crew about our Navy heritage and to show them why, every day, they were expected to live up to it.

Benfold was in the Arleigh Burke class of destroyers, named for the famous commodore who helped win the crucial Battle of Leyte Gulf against the Japanese in the Philippines. Burke, who also distinguished himself in the Korean War and served as President Dwight D. Eisenhower's chief of naval operations, later commissioned a painting of the battle and had 750 prints made. He gave Defense Secretary William Perry the first copy.

When I was leaving Perry's office after serving as his military assistant, he asked if there was anything he could do for me, and I asked if he could spare the print. He was happy to give it to me. And although it would have looked great in my cabin, I hung it on the mess deck where the whole crew could see it. Then I told them about Arleigh Burke and what he had meant to the Navy, so they would know how *Benfold*'s class came to be named and what a great hero and leader Burke was. They got the message that they were, in a sense, Burke's descendants and should strive to emulate their forebear. That print forms the backdrop for the cover of this book.

All clear-thinking leaders know that money alone can't buy job satisfaction. As leaders, we are receptive to giving people meaning and purpose in their jobs, solid reasons to get up in the morning and speed to work. But how do you turn these abstract words into living deeds? How do you pass out daily meaning to jaded skeptics?

This chapter describes the purpose patrol I created and personally carried out every single day that I commanded *Benfold*. The whole idea was to give my sailors an ever bigger context for their work: a sense of American naval history, the ship's mission, our core values, the all-fleet prizes we could (and did) win if we tried.

Whatever your business, our experiences and the lessons gleaned from them are easily translatable to the business world. As the cases I've recently studied clearly demonstrate, these techniques will do wonders for morale in any venue.

LOOK BEHIND YOU FOR INSPIRATION
(AND MORE).

I got the idea for educating my crew about the Navy's heritage when I worked for Dr. Perry. John Hagen, the master chief petty officer of the Navy at the time, was my inspiration. John and I talked about the fact that sailors today seem to know little if anything about the Navy's rich history and traditions. He told me that he was going to push for heritage training to be part of the curriculum at our Great Lakes recruit training center in Chicago, and I brought that idea to *Benfold*.

At my request, a local San Diego businessman gave us the PBS film documentary *Victory in the Pacific*, and we showed the DVD on our closed-circuit TV system. Then, as we sailed across the Pacific on our way to the Middle East, we steamed through waters that had been the site of great World War II naval battles. We held seminars before reaching the sites, telling our sailors about each battle and spelling out the strategy each side used and why it had or hadn't worked.

I'll never forget the morning we crossed the Sibuyan Sea, where the Battle of Leyte Gulf, the largest naval battle in modern history, was fought from October 23 to October 26, 1944.

I had arranged to leave the battle group to make a detour so we could go through the islands at sunrise, reliving the battle our ships endured. We sailed through the San Bernardino Strait as the sun was coming up and served breakfast on the flight deck. The experience was incredibly moving. For the first time, I felt that many of my sailors were starting to understand the importance of our heritage. Their recognition would play a big part in making *Benfold* the best ship in the Navy.

For any organization that has been around for a while, heritage can be a powerful tool for leadership. I've recently been working with the District of Columbia Metro Police. Its new chief, Cathy Lanier, realized that her recruits at the academy weren't being trained in the history and traditions of the D.C. police force, so she has started a program to teach them about the heroes upon whose shoulders they stand.

Businesses are taking similar actions. A case in point is Xerox. Few such iconic companies have found themselves in a corporate hole as deep as the one Xerox occupied near the end of 2000. The once-swaggering company had lost its way, beset by stronger competition, a weakening economy, an accounting scandal, and a series of questionable management decisions. For the first time in its history, Xerox was losing money.

Debt had risen to a mountainous $19 billion, revenues were shrinking at a double-digit pace, and the value of Xerox's stock had been sawed in half. As longtime director Vernon Jordan related, the pivotal moment came at a meeting called to discuss how Xerox would file for bankruptcy in the coming week.

For nearly an hour, the lawyers, consultants, financial advisers, and public-relations people discussed the action as a done deal, a no-brainer. Finally, Anne Mulcahy, the twenty-four-year veteran who had recently been named CEO, pushed back her chair, stood up, and declared: "This company is not filing for bankruptcy. I realize that might be the prudent thing to do, but this is Xerox. We have a legacy to uphold. Xerox will not fail on our watch."

From where Jordan sat, Mulcahy was invoking the core values of Xerox: "She did it for Xerox people, who all believe they are a part of an ongoing experiment to demonstrate that good business and good values are not only compatible but synergistic, that good guys and good gals can, in fact, finish first." And in Mulcahy's telling, it was the Xerox employees' faith in those core values that underpinned the near-miraculous turnaround over which she presided.

Within four years, profit was nearing $1 billion, the mountain of debt had eroded by half, costs had been reduced by $2 billion, and the stock value had doubled. "Our employees told us they would do damn near anything to save the company," Mulcahy recalled later, and they were true to their word. "They did an incredible job."

Mulcahy kept her side of the implicit bargain, too. As Jordan remembered it, "Anne insisted that the company's core values not be compromised, even as Xerox struggled to survive. Xerox continued to invest in the nonprofit sector, protect the environment, volunteer in the community, and treat its employees with respect and dignity," he said. In Jordan's estimation, Xerox is a special company that had the good fortune to be led by a special person, one who understood and valued the company's heritage.

LOOK TO THE STARS FOR CLARITY OF PURPOSE.

Before Michael Bleier became interested in the management side of the wholesale heating and cooling business his father started back in 1980, he was content to sit by as, first, his father and, then, his older brother Dan ran the company from a position of power far removed from the company's rank-and-file. No one ever talked about whether the company's employees were content and focused on a common goal. And a mission was something an astronaut went on, or one of those old Spanish churches that line the coast of California.

Then Michael, an engineer by training who felt most at home with systems, had an epiphany of sorts: He realized that Able would never become a superior company unless it adopted a mission and convinced its employees of the mission's value. And the only way to do that was through good leadership.

But though Michael was full of excitement about what he envisioned, he had no earthly idea how to bring his vision to life. The projects he started were "pretty ugly," he recalls, nothing more than fuzzy ideas, fuzzy goals, and, as one might expect, fuzzy commitment from the Able workforce. That's when he began studying other businesses that had reached for the stars and become stars themselves. These benchmarks, he says, gave him ideas for "freeing up creativity, freeing up information, and freeing up our people to make great decisions."

But before Michael could apply anything he was learning, he first had to take a cold, hard look at Able Distributors. "We are a wholesaler," he told me, "so our primary function or mission is to be able to identify, purchase, warehouse, and, ultimately, sell— hopefully for a profit—materials." But guess what? Wholesaling was the one area where the company was doing a not-so-great job. "Our warehouses were a little tired," Michael confessed. "Our showrooms were a little tired. Our inventory systems weren't really systems. They sort of just grew out of this organic idea that the better you buy something, the more money you're going to make."

In other words, Able was really good at buying products, but it couldn't keep track of them properly or store them efficiently or display them pleasingly or retrieve them expeditiously. All of which negated its fabulous buying skills. What to do? Michael decided the company had to make operational excellence its mission, and it had to make the whys and the hows crystal clear to its workforce.

"I saw how important it is to create a culture where people aren't fighting against our mission," he told me. "Our mission was to deliver an exceptional experience, and inventory control was a major component of customer service. It really didn't matter if the truck was on time. It really didn't matter how well we answered the phone or how cool our T-shirts were if we didn't have the ten items a contractor needed, because we wouldn't be in business much longer."

With those thoughts in mind, Michael began redesigning the whole company. All of its warehouses have been reorganized; they've been mapped and bin locations identified, and everything has been computerized. Procedural changes have been made and analyzed and their benefits defined and documented. Staff training has been stepped up and procedures put down in writing. And all the new procedures and processes are measured for their contribution to the success of the mission.

BROADCAST WHAT YOU ARE, AND WHAT YOU WANT TO BE.

On *Benfold*, I used the PA system so often that the sailors called me Mega Mike. Every time I spoke to the crew, I had my network of spies—trusted officers or my chief petty officer—circulating among the sailors to gauge their reaction to what I was saying. I wanted to make sure my message was getting through, and I also needed to know if I was crossing the line of what is appropriate for a captain to say. Sometimes I strayed from talking about the duties of a sailor to discuss ethical issues. And based on the feedback I got, the crew seemed to agree that while religion doesn't belong in the workplace, ethics is a legitimate part of a captain's message.

When we pulled into a foreign port after a long time at sea, for instance, I'd talk about safe sex and the danger of contracting or spreading HIV, the human immunodeficiency virus that can lead to AIDS. Many of my sailors were married. I didn't think what people did in their hotel rooms was any of my business, but problems arise when everyone knows a sailor is hooking up and a spouse back home gets wind of the cheating. So I told them, "I'm not here to be your religious adviser, but I want you to know that if you are married, you should think about honoring your marriage vows. And if you don't, make sure you deal with it privately."

The master chief came back and told me that sailors were nodding their heads; they had gotten and appreciated the message. Sometimes what happens on business trips is given a wink or a nod. Leaders need to know that condoning and celebrating ethical lapses creates a bad culture that spills over into the business, as the Enron crowd made all too clear.

Technology has created a great mission-communication opportunity for business leaders, especially for those whose people are physically dispersed and working in virtual offices. Blogs, for instance, give CEOs a new way to make sure their message is getting out and to get feedback and fresh ideas from their people. A CEO can come in on a Monday morning and write a two-paragraph summary of priorities for the week. Then the staff can follow up with what they're doing to meet the agenda, what's working and what's not, and suggestions for new ways to do it better.

When Anne Mulcahy was fighting to save Xerox, blogs hadn't yet been invented. So to spread her vision and clarify the situation for the company's 70,000 people, she traveled all over the corporate empire for face-to-face talks and "town meetings" with large groups of employees. She told them what had gone wrong and how she meant to fix it; more important, she told them what they could do to help. She ended each session by telling them it was their choice: "If you don't have an appetite for it, leave. If you do, roll up your sleeves and get to work."

At those meetings, Anne said, she expected the burning question to be whether Xerox could survive. Instead, the employees wanted to know what the company would look like when the crisis was over. "It was this amazing vote of confidence that I took as a very good sign," she recalled.

But instead of writing up a vision statement or preparing a typical brochure, she ordered up a fictitious *Wall Street Journal* story, dated four years in the future, describing the Xerox of 2005. "It turned out to be just a rallying point in the company," she said. "People got it. It built a sense of optimism, and it provided a road map for where we could take the company. It was an important part of giving people a goalpost to go after."

The way Xerox's people rallied around the cause, Anne said, was "the critical element of the turnaround. The strategy was okay, roughly right. The implementation plan was okay. But I would say that the people really aligned themselves around a common set of objectives, and that really was the magic." I would add that the magic worked mainly because Anne had communicated her vision so completely and clearly.

UNDERSTANDING IS BETTER THAN TRUST.

Sometimes your people will do what you ask because they trust you; you ordered them to do it, so they do. Trust as a motivator is better than fear of discipline, but neither one is as good as making it clear to your people why the job is necessary. I failed at that on a deployment to the Middle East in 1997.

It was a year after the bombing of the Khobar Towers in Saudi Arabia, which killed nineteen American servicemen. I had gone there with Defense Secretary Perry to see the damage, and I clearly remember standing in the 400-foot-wide crater left by the bomb. What I figured out that day was that we and our enemies had learned different lessons from the first Iraq war. We realized we could never have enough planes, tanks, and ships; they realized they would never get enough planes, tanks, and ships, so they had to try something else—and that something else turned out to be terrorism.

When *Benfold* went to the Middle East a year later, I was a raving lunatic about pier security, making sure that trucks carrying explosives couldn't get close to the pier and that we had gunners in place to shoot any small boats that might come alongside. My officers thought I was crazy. They didn't see the threat that I saw, and the unpleasant conditions didn't help their understanding.

Amid temperatures that reached 130 degrees Fahrenheit, my sailors had to sit out there manning guns and inspecting garbage trucks and Dumpsters before their drivers could come onto the pier. It was awful work, and both the officers and crew thought it a wasted effort. And when I shared my anxieties with a commodore in port, he e-mailed me to say, "You're being paranoid." He reminded me that there had never been a terrorist attack on a

Navy ship in port, and there was no intelligence indicating otherwise. But I felt strongly about it; I had done the what-if exercises, figured out our potential weaknesses, and worked out tactics to offset them.

Three years later, after the bombing of USS *Cole* in Yemen, I got e-mails from about fifty of my sailors telling me they now understood why I had given those orders. Their level of trust in me had risen, and I appreciated that. But the fact was that I had failed to get the idea across when I needed to make it clear.

FOCUS ON WHAT MATTERS AND IGNORE THE REST.

When people lack confidence and courage, they retreat to doing only what they find comfortable. It's true in the Navy and it's true in business. And in both cases, paperwork often turns out to be the comforting diversion. I saw many officers and captains who holed up in their cabins doing paperwork all day long. I had the advantage of working for the secretary of defense, which gave me a larger perspective.

On a ship, people operate at sea level, and they are obsessed with paperwork because they think that's what people higher up are doing. But, as I saw firsthand, people at the highest levels don't obsess over paperwork; they obsess over the results. I learned to determine what paperwork was important and what wasn't, so I could prioritize it. If it wasn't important, I didn't want my officers wasting their time on it.

Some of our paperwork involved evaluations, which were important because careers depend on them. But much of the rest was pointless. Among the most common time-wasters were letters from people preying on the sailors, like loan sharks who demanded outrageous rates of interest on payday loans. Obviously, such problems had to be dealt with, but not by generating more paperwork.

One such "businessman" operated a camera shop right outside the gates of the Great Lakes recruit training center in Chicago. He sold sailors five-year plans carrying huge monthly payments just for buying film and getting it developed. When the sailors got fed up and stopped sending this guy money, he wrote letters to the captain demanding payment. I farmed the letters out to the department heads and division officers. But my biggest concern was how to put this scum out of business. History is full of people trying to take advantage of young men and women serving our country, and I think it's deplorable.

I sent the sailors to the command master chief for financial counseling and told the chief to call the camera shop's owner with this message: Either rip up the contracts or find that your shop has been put off limits by the commander at the training center. I honestly didn't know if I had the authority to get that done, but I would have tried. The owner ripped up the contracts.

Much of the Navy's paperwork is the flotsam and jetsam of a 230-year history. No one ever gives it the commonsense check: "Is this still necessary?" My yardstick was whether the paper had anything to do with our ability to carry out our mission. If it didn't, it went into the circular file.

One piece of paper that was truly crucial to our mission was the "binnacle list" of sick and injured crewmen that is provided every day by the chief corpsman. In the old days, the list was posted on the binnacle, which houses the ship's compass, to make sure the captain saw it. To me, it was just as important as knowing the state of my budget or how much fuel and water I had onboard— and I came by that reverence after working for a disagreeable old admiral in Subic Bay.

Paul Butcher had responsibility for all of the ships in the western Pacific and was widely disliked. But having come to the Navy as an enlisted man, Admiral Butcher held officers to a higher standard when it came to taking care of the crew. When a sailor on a ship under Butcher's flag died of an illness that could have been cured with proper medical treatment, the captain was stunned when Butcher relieved him of command. Why such a harsh response? Because it turned out that the captain hadn't even known the sailor was sick.

That made an impression on me. I realized that nothing is more important to a captain than the health of his crew. On *Benfold*, my chief corpsman came to me every day that one of my sailors was receiving treatment to discuss the case. And I always asked if the corpsman felt comfortable dealing with the case or wanted help from a doctor. Corpsmen are somewhat like nurse-practitioners, although they are not registered nurses; they can put in a temporary filling in a dental emergency, and I've heard of corpsmen who performed appendectomies with radioed instructions. But at sea, the corpsman is all the medical care there is.

I knew that Reese Olger, *Benfold's* chief corpsman, put the health of the crew first. I had complete trust in his medical skills and knew he wouldn't hesitate to ask for a doctor's help if he needed it. Reese was the finest corpsman I met during my Navy career, and I was lucky to have him. My crew was even luckier.

NEVER ASSUME THAT PEOPLE KNOW YOUR COMPANY'S CORE VALUES.

On *Benfold* I learned that, like the job of motivating the crew, clarifying what we were all about boiled down mainly to a teaching job. Any leader constantly has to repeat and reinforce the mission message, the organization's values and heritage, and the importance of the small details that go into every phase of the work.

I took my cue from Bill Walsh. Passed over for several head coaching jobs, the legendary leader of the 49ers once wrote that "owners wanted someone who'd yell and scream and whip their players into submission, but I don't believe that's how to coach. My approach is to teach, because players need to be prepared mentally to play the sophisticated football of the nineties. And the longer you're in the game, the more you see how significant the details and teaching and education are."

In many cases, the first thing a leader must teach is the core values of the organization she leads—and she may be astonished at how few of her people understand them. At Tec Labs, for instance, Steve Smith decided in 1997 to remind his staff of the company's "Midwest Farm Belt work ethic." He had been naively assuming that his new hires understood that the work ethic was part of the mission. "And, my goodness," Steve told me, "they absolutely didn't. It broke my heart."

It was probably his fault, he said. Perhaps he didn't give new employees enough information, or maybe he didn't work hard enough at getting his points across. Whatever the reason, Steve embarked on a quest to clarify the company's mission.

Ironically, things got worse before they got better. Steve discovered, for instance, that his "no problem" mantra—a leading candidate for inclusion in any statement of Tec's core values—had been completely misinterpreted by one longtime employee. "My idea of a no-problem attitude," he explained to me, "is you come to me and you say you need help with this project. If I can help you, I'll say, 'Okay, no problem.' If I can't, I'll say, 'No problem, but let's either figure out how to solve this problem together or find somebody else who can help you.'"

But what the misguided employee thought a "no problem" attitude meant was: "It's not my problem. It's your problem. And I can't help you, no problem." Although otherwise competent and cheerful, this employee wasn't a team player in Tec's value system. And even after the meaning of Steve's mantra was clarified for her, she still wasn't going to change. But at that point, she herself knew she didn't fit in, and eventually she left of her own accord.

Marc Jacobson told me a similar story. "When you make a dramatic change in an operation, when you decide that the past does not equal the future and you are going to make changes, not everybody is going to make the trip. And that's okay," he said, "because one bad person can destroy everything you've built up."

After Marc decided to refocus his financial services firm on giving clients an exceptional experience, he set to work changing the mind-set of his staff members. One fellow refused to budge. He told Marc that he had joined the company for what it was before, not for what Marc wanted it to be. He said he had no intention of making the required changes. What's more, he disliked everyone else in the office and would not work with them.

This behavior left Marc with no choice: "I told him that he had a week to change his mind or he had to go. Not one person, including myself, is more important than the operation."

The anti-boss employee didn't need a week to decide. He repeated his position then and there. Case closed. Marc fired the man on the spot and walked him out of the office with the entire staff looking on. It was a defining moment for the agency. Marc had never asked his people what they liked or didn't like about their jobs, but their answer was clear as the mutineer disappeared. "What a relief," they sighed.

"Your staff is a lot smarter than you think," Marc told me. I already knew that.

MONITOR THE QUALITY OF FAILURE.

Sometimes the thing that needs clarifying is simply how to win. Perhaps the greatest lesson Bill Walsh learned—and taught his players—was that failure beats you only if you let it. His first season with the 49ers, with two wins and fourteen defeats, was just as disastrous as his predecessor's last season. The next year ended with only a 6–9 record, and a coach with a less tolerant owner might well have been fired. Even worse, a less cerebral coach might have thought he deserved to be fired.

But Walsh knew that the scores that year were less lopsided than the previous season's, and the team's offense had lifted itself from twenty-seventh in the league to sixth. "The quality of failure had fundamentally changed," he said, and that clarified the extent of the problem.

"When you're determined to use failure as a school for success," Walsh noted later, "you'll find that it's easier to hold a strategic course and refine the plan, rather than constantly second-guessing yourself. Panic subsides, along with depression, embarrassment, humiliation, and all the other unhappy by-products of perceiving failure as an unmitigated disaster."

The next year, Walsh's third as head coach, the team kept its cool even while struggling at mid-season with a 6–5 record and two consecutive losses—but that was also the first year they went on to win the Super Bowl. "We had learned to win by learning about losing," Walsh explained. "We had learned that failure beats you only if you let it."

As you know by now, clarifying the mission covers a good deal of ground. A leader must define the organization's goals and spell out why they matter. A leader must convey the core values and heritage that keep the organization going. Leaders must motivate their people to achieve their personal best and see to it that they understand their responsibilities. Leaders must set up feedback mechanisms to make sure all these messages get across, and they must stress, clearly and constantly, the importance of winning. But leaders must also be clear in their own minds about the right risks to take and when to take them. That's the subject of the next chapter.

CHAPTER 7

SAIL CLOSE TO THE WIND

TAKING THE RIGHT RISKS

RISK IS A PART OF LIVING. IT'S THE ESSENCE OF THE MILI-tary life and equally fundamental to business. It is also the precursor to reward. Like turtles and giraffes, we can't get any-where without sticking our necks out. But, as I learned during my Navy career, the inevitability of risk doesn't sanction recklessness. Learning to take the right risks in the right way is paramount to survival and success. Sure, there are heroes like Edward Benfold, who picked up the incoming grenades and charged the enemy soldiers, killing them at the cost of his own life. But a dead hero is still dead. Desperate gambles should be undertaken only when you're pinned down and have no other option for getting out alive.

Good leaders always calculate the odds and minimize the risk by having backups in place. Above all, they never take a risk that doesn't offer a worthwhile reward. How do you calculate your odds of succeeding in a dangerous situation? By gaining a thorough understanding of the risk you're running and an equally thorough understanding of what you'll do if something goes wrong.

A captain trying to navigate out of San Diego harbor, for instance, needs to know ahead of time that there are bends in the channel that can cause the unwary to run aground. You can get away with letting the less-experienced officer of the deck steer the ship across the center of the harbor, but if you let him round the bends without the proper training, you're risking your ship and your reputation as a navigator for no good reason.

I certainly took my share of risks as *Benfold*'s captain, but I seldom stuck my neck out without first calculating the odds of winning, and, even then, I at least partly hedged my bets in case something went wrong. Questioning orders or asking for reconsideration of a superior officer's decision could have left me teetering on the edge of insubordination. But, to better my odds of success, I made sure I had a pretty clear idea of how the people I was dealing with would react before I pressed them to buy into my alternative as a better choice.

In a way, dealing with risk is like sailing a boat upwind, tacking back and forth to get where you want to go. You want to sail as close to the wind as you can, to take advantage of every last breath of it and shorten the zigzag distance you travel. But if you get too close, the sail will stop pulling, and you'll be dead in the water. You have to develop a feel for exactly how close to the wind you can get, to maximize the boat's performance. It's the same with calculating risks.

In practice, of course, it's not so easy to calculate every possible element of risk. But you can usually anticipate the main problems and try to work around them or fix them before they become insurmountable. When I decided to train Petty Officer Michael Murray to be officer of the deck, for example (a story I told in Chapter 5), it was, in my opinion, clearly a risk worth taking.

In the first place, I needed to free up my senior officers for more important duty, and second, the dangers associated with promoting Michael didn't seem all that great. What was the worst that could happen? Well, Michael could have turned out to be lousy at the job. He could easily have overplayed his hand in giving orders to officers, thereby creating resentment. But I would have spotted the problems during his training, and the experiment would have come to an end right then and there. As it was, Michael clearly saw the pitfalls of the position I was putting him in and welcomed my suggestions about how to be diplomatic. In the end, he won the crew's respect with his superior ship-driving ability, and the risk paid off just as I thought it would.

Some leaders have an intuitive sense of how to calculate risks, deal with the potential pitfalls, and, eventually, rake in the jackpot with a winning hand. But most of us have to make a few mistakes, sometimes big and embarrassing ones, before we can get a true feel for the consequences of the risks we're confronting and how to deal with them beforehand. To help you hone your sense of risk and avoid the really big ones, here are a few lessons I've learned along the way.

KNOW WHICH RISKS CAN BE HEDGED.

Once you understand what can go wrong, you can usually mitigate the risk. Take the time I wanted to make a show of my confidence in the crew and, particularly, in a junior officer, Lieutenant Jerry Olin. I decided to let Jerry get the ship under way by himself, moving it from the pier for a major inspection at sea. Unmooring and moving away from the pier can be a tricky maneuver, particularly for someone who's never done it before; if too much power is applied or if the wind and current are allowed to take control, you can do serious damage to a very expensive piece of Uncle Sam's equipment. And the captain who authorizes an inexperienced sailor to perform the maneuver is the one whose head is on the block if something bad happens. But Jerry pulled it off without a hitch, and I was proud of him.

What Jerry and everyone else onboard didn't know, though, was that I had a Plan B if something went wrong. When a ship leaves the pier, a tugboat is always standing by in case it's needed. I made sure that the best harbor pilot in San Diego was aboard the tug that day, and he knew that if Jerry got into any trouble, he was to waste no time in using the tug to push *Benfold* back against the pier until I could get to the bridge.

I hedged a risk in a different way in my time with William Perry. I had taken a flight on NAOC, the National Airborne Operations Center, the Boeing 747 that had been outfitted as a command post for the entire national defense in case of nuclear attack. In the Cold War years, it had been in-flight twenty-four hours a day, ready to pick up the secretary of defense and perhaps the president in case of emergency. But it was now seven years since the Cold War had ended, and there had been no investment in updating its 1970s technology. That was a risk in itself, since no one knew whether it was capable of performing its mission. I wanted Dr. Perry to see for himself how obsolete it was, and at my suggestion, he decided to fly in NAOC on his next trip.

But that decision posed another risk. Washington was in the grip of the flap called Travelgate, which centered on government officials flying around like potentates. Official travel costs, particularly in the Defense Department, were under scrutiny. The NAOC cost considerably more to operate than the plane Perry usually used, and if a reporter found out about this flight, it could be more fuel for the Travelgate fire.

So, at our regular morning meeting, I spoke up about it. I felt that speaking up was a risk in itself. As the junior person at the meeting, I hadn't said anything for five or six months. I was actually shaking as I started to talk, worrying that Perry might brush off my point or that I'd be embarrassed.

But I felt strongly enough about it that I plunged ahead, pointing out the danger of unfavorable publicity that could come from flying around in such a large plane. To my great relief, Dr. Perry agreed with me and directed that we tell the press what we were doing and get the story out on our terms. From then on I felt free to talk in the morning meeting.

We invited the press to tour the plane before the trip, and the resulting stories told how the secretary was making sure NAOC was up to its mission. Once he had flown in it, he knew that it wasn't, and the advance publicity had prepared the groundwork for his program to upgrade the plane so that it could actually be used to command the nation's armed forces. Today, the secretary of defense has a means of directing our military in a crisis using state-of-the-art technology.

Brian Scudamore hedges his bets in much the same ways when allowing his people to take risks at 1-800-GOT-JUNK?. "We take chances as much as we can to try people, to see how they do," he told me. But "we're not going to put someone in a leadership position who would be overwhelmed or expose the company to some massive setback." Before giving untried people new responsibilities, he continued, "we talk to them about some of the challenges they might face, some of the frustrations. Afterward, we put them through a debriefing so they know how they can do better next time, and we all learn from the process."

DISAGREE WITHOUT DISRESPECT.

I came up with a way to disagree with my boss's decisions without getting into trouble. I'd get on the radio and ask for an instant replay, just as a coach in the National Football League can throw a red flag to question a referee's decision and ask for a review of the videotape. It's a risky thing to do, both in the NFL and in the Navy, because if you're wrong, there's a significant penalty. The NFL coach loses a timeout, and he can't throw another red flag for the rest of the half. A captain who's wrong will probably be ignored the next time. I was right nine out of ten times—and I'd say I was right the tenth time, too, even though I lost the decision.

My luck ran out when *Benfold* was accompanying *Gary* and *Harry W. Hill* on another submarine-hunting exercise off Honolulu. The captain of *Gary* was in charge of the exercise, but two days before it was to start, he hadn't distributed a plan of action. I saw a vacuum waiting to be filled and called in my junior operations specialist and my junior sonar men. Once again, as described in Chapter 5, I told them to think creatively and devise a plan never tried before to catch the submarine. They came up with a brilliant strategy, one I never would have thought of. It was a far better plan than the earlier one.

The traditional sub-hunting unit has one high-value ship and two escorts. The high-value ship in this exercise was *Hill*, which had the commodore aboard. The conventional plan, used by the Navy for half a century, called for *Hill* to steam in the middle of the formation with an escort on either side.

But our guys wanted to disguise *Hill* as a freighter by altering the signature of her propeller and having her steam off on the far side of the operating area. The sub's captain would be wondering where the third destroyer was and probably wouldn't try anything until he had figured it out. Meanwhile, *Benfold* and *Gary* would deploy towed-array sonar systems with hydrophones that could determine the depth of the lurking submarine, and we could then destroy it with simulated torpedoes.

We forwarded the plan to the commodore just as *Gary's* captain was sending out his plan. Sure enough, it was the same plan the Navy had been using since 1945. The commodore went with *Gary's* plan anyway, and when I asked for an instant replay, he still backed the captain who was supposed to be running the exercise.

The architects of our plan were in my cabin when I challenged the commodore, and they knew I was heartbroken to learn their scheme wouldn't be given a chance. But they knew I had tried. And in the upshot, the submarine sank all three of us in the first ninety minutes of the exercise. It was like a turkey shoot. Deep down, I didn't much care. We had done our best during the exercise, of course, but I didn't take ownership of the failure because I knew the plan was a loser from the get-go and a better one was available. Better or not, our plan was deep-sixed by tradition.

The lesson here applies in business, too. You can have the best organization and the best people in the world, but if you have a lousy business plan, you're going to fail, and no one will take ownership of the defeat. Tradition is no excuse for conducting business as usual when there is a better way.

AVOID A RISK THAT'S NOT WORTH TAKING.

One of the hardest lessons to teach is to steer clear of a risk that isn't worth taking. I learned that as a boy growing up in Altoona, Pennsylvania. I was charged with painting the trim on our brick house during summer vacations. Like many a young man, I was in a hurry and didn't take time to put down a drop cloth to catch the drips and splatters.

My mother, bless her, raised hell when I dripped paint on the bricks as I painted around the windows. It's almost impossible to get paint out of the porous brick, so the stain is visible forever. I only made that mistake once. From then on, inciting my mother's wrath was not a risk I wanted to take. Ever since, I've used a drop cloth when painting anything.

But sailors never use drop cloths, and they always spill paint. If they're painting a fire hydrant, they drop red paint on the deck, which then requires them to repaint the deck gray, and, invariably, they spill gray paint on the black nonskid surface. When all is said and done, the simple job of painting the hydrant turns into a three-stage painting marathon. It was a standing joke on the ship that if the captain spotted a sailor with a paint can, he would order the sailor to get a drop cloth.

My crew got a kick out of my unvarying response, but it sent a signal: We don't take pointless risks, we do things right the first time, and we pay close attention to detail even in small things. In business, as in sports or the military, it's all about executing the small things in an outstanding manner.

My mother didn't sail with me on *Benfold*, but Command Master Chief Scheeler filled in for her.

Essentially, the command master is the senior enlisted member of the ship, reporting directly to, and working with, the commanding officer. He or she works on behalf of all of the ship's enlisted personnel and is their direct liaison to the commanding officer. But besides being responsible for the health, welfare, morale, and training of the enlisted personnel, a huge job all by itself, the command master chief also serves as something of a sounding board for the captain in terms of the ship's policies and procedures.

As Bob Scheeler himself described it, the command master "is the guy who tells the emperor he has no clothes. And when the emperor says, 'Okay, I don't have any clothes on but I'm still going out in the middle of the street to lead the parade,' the command master carries on like it's his idea and supports the emperor."

No matter what, Scheeler could walk into my cabin, close the door, and tell me that what I was doing, or proposed to do, was not right—and (shades of my mother) he exercised that option more than once. Like the time I told you about in Chapter 4, when he objected to bringing beer onboard. Scheeler felt that mixing alcohol with a healthy crew of red-blooded male and female sailors who had been stuck at sea for six months was a risk not worth taking. I appreciated his concern for my career and I knew that he was just looking out for me in this instance. I didn't take his advice and never regretted it.

But Scheeler's misgivings proved to be right on target when I decided to make my contact with the crew more informal. The

Navy stands on tradition, in most cases, for good reason. But the age-old formality between the captain and the crew began to wear on me. Every time I strolled around the deck or entered the mess decks or wandered into a work area, everything came to a sudden stop as the crew members came to attention and saluted. I hated the loss of productivity. So I told the command master that I wanted to change all that. I wanted an easier, less-strained relationship with the crew, and I wanted the work to go on.

Scheeler tried to talk me out of it, explaining that relaxing the formality would blur the lines of command, which could prove disastrous in an emergency. The commanding officer may have to take his ship and his crew into harm's way, and the crew must follow orders without a moment's hesitation. They must do what they are told simply because the captain says so. Questioning orders puts lives and missions at risk. But I was so uncomfortable with the extreme formality and loss of productivity that I didn't listen to reason.

The master chief responded like all good chiefs do. He accepted my decision as his own and supported me in my resolve to stop this business of coming to attention at the mere sight of me (much to the chagrin of the ship's thirty-five chief petty officers, as I later learned; they were traditionalists, too). Before long, though, I had to admit that the command master chief was right. The yes-sirs and no-sirs degenerated into uh-huhs and yeah-mans. And just as Scheeler had predicted, the relaxed standards were creeping into other areas. The crew treated me more like a daytime boss than a figure holding absolute 24/7 authority over them.

So I called Scheeler in to reverse my previous decision. "As much as I don't want to have to do this," I told him, "we have to go back to the formality." I had accepted a risk not worth taking, and one that could have brought disaster to *Benfold*. There were no "I told you so"s from the master chief. He simply reinstated an age-old naval tradition that correctly demands a certain aloofness between the captain and the crew.

MAKE SURE YOU HAVE BACKUPS.

For a leader, the simplest kind of what-if scenario involves losing people—whether to enemy action, or sickness, or merely transfers to other postings. As I've said before, I aimed to have *Benfold* four deep in people who could handle every job onboard. But it was astonishing how many commanders were casual to the point of carelessness about training backups.

Near the end of my time on one ship, only three of us were qualified to be officer of the deck, which meant we stood four hours on the bridge and had eight hours off. But when I left unexpectedly—I had been chosen to be an admiral's aide—the captain hadn't trained any backups, so the two remaining officers had to work six hours on and six off. That's brutal, because you never get enough uninterrupted sleep. After three weeks of this at sea, they came back zombies. They were both pissed off at me for leaving. But their real quarrel was with the captain, for not having thought: What if?

DON'T SHUN RISKS.

Arguably, the biggest risk of all may be creating a climate in which people are afraid to take any risks. That happened in the military in the early 1990s, when a budget-balancing plan started by the first President Bush and carried out by President Clinton reduced the armed forces from 2.1 million men and women to just 1.2 million on active duty.

Shrinking the services was painful. There were selection boards to figure out who had to be retired early and how not to let people re-enlist. In practice, it meant that any officer who had even one small blemish on his record got chosen for early retirement. That led to a very risk-averse atmosphere. People didn't want to rock the boat and risk ending their careers. Rather than take any initiatives, they would lie low in the weeds and let other people get black marks.

It was a terrible signal to send. We stopped trying new things, and as a result, we lost our cutting edge in preparing for future threats. We paid for that, I'm convinced, on 9/11, and then we had to play catch-up.

One of the key assets we lost in the Navy was the roster of senior captains, the seasoned veterans who were never going to make admiral but had the institutional knowledge and made the machinery run in every major port we had. They weren't strategic geniuses, but they did the unsexy blocking and tackling: getting ships repaired, making sure training was done on schedule. Without them, the machinery started breaking down.

Luckily for me, I had had my experience in Dr. Perry's office. I knew what success was, and I had achieved it; my next promotion wasn't what was driving me. So I had a kind of immunity to the risk-averse climate, and I could continue to push the envelope. Given that general climate, I think a lot of my bosses respected me for it.

I admit I was counting on that, a bit at least, the day I pulled off my most public display of insubordination.

It was in the Persian Gulf, and we were about to launch a cruise missile attack against Iraq. The admiral had called a planning conference on the *Nimitz* aircraft carrier, and a helicopter was sent around to pick up a representative from each ship. When the chopper got to *Benfold*, we tied it down, refueled it, and gave its crew a bite to eat. Then someone from the carrier called over and told us there wasn't enough room on the chopper for my representative. We were disinvited to the conference, not by the admiral or his staff, but by a logistician.

That rubbed me the wrong way. I was determined to have a place at the table. *Benfold* had more Tomahawk missiles than any ship in the Gulf, and we were the centerpiece of the attack. I wasn't about to let some staffer on *Nimitz* keep me from sending my officer. I knew damn well this wasn't coming from the admiral or his staff; it was way below their radar screen. If no one from my ship showed up, they weren't going to know the reason. They were going to think we didn't care enough to come.

I was holding an ace: Once the helicopter was on my deck, it couldn't take off without my permission. So I said I wouldn't give it until my representative was onboard. For forty-five minutes, while the staff on the carrier fumed over what to do, the hostage chopper sat on my landing pad with its rotor spinning. Finally they relented and let me send a representative. Some other ship had to be left out. The next day there was a cartoon in the carrier's underground newspaper showing me holding the helicopter hostage.

That was a risk for me, and I confess that in the heat of the moment I didn't fully calculate it. But I knew that I wasn't defying the admiral or his staff, just some logistical bean counter on the carrier. And if anyone had called me on it, I would have argued that *Benfold*'s representative needed to be there to make sure the mission was flawless, and that the admiral hadn't been well served by his minions who were trying to keep us away. In the end, the word that came back to me was that most people on the carrier thought it was neat that I had the *cojones* to do something like that.

Calculating risks is one thing, and deciding which risks to accept is another. Both are cool, intellectual exercises. But actually sticking your head into the lion's mouth is altogether different. It demands courage, which some people have in large measure and others lack. Courage is also an indispensable quality of leadership, and it shows up in every action a leader takes as she or he shows people the power of personal example. That's the subject of the next and final chapter.

CHAPTER 8

FLY YOUR TRUE COLORS

Leading by Example and Getting Results

⚓ Like ships, leaders leave a wake behind them as they pass through an organization. All eyes are on them; everything they do, no matter how insignificant, is taken as a signal, and their people follow their example, for good or ill. Whatever they intend, and no matter what they write in memos or say in speeches, the true quality of their leadership is measured by the example they set.

You'd think the Navy and businesses would focus intently on teaching effective leadership. What could be more important for an institution that prepares people to stay cool in life-and-death situations? But the Navy, like most other large organizations, could do much better. Even at the Naval Academy, we were taught only the theory of leadership, not actually how to lead.

And as for leading by example, most of the teachers and administrators seemed to have a penchant for doing the exact opposite of what great leaders do. The environment was very oppressive, and no mistakes were allowed. By definition, learning begins with making mistakes. But we were forced to operate with a totally unrealistic zero-defect mentality.

Even when I got command of a ship, the Navy didn't make it easy to lead. No one suggested how I might deal with the dozens of challenges I would face as the captain of a ship. Any kind of help and advice would have been appreciated. Had the Navy constructed a tool kit of leadership lessons, I probably wouldn't have used them all right away, but it would have given me confidence to know that guidance was there when I needed it. Such a tool kit would have been good for the Navy as well as for the captains. A paragraph from the chief of naval operations saying this is how I want you to handle such and such a situation would have gone a long way toward making sure that every captain was doing things the way the chief wanted.

As it was, I got so used to charting my own course without help from experienced leaders that I unconsciously accepted the void as just another example of the way things work. And having adopted the sink-or-swim mentality, I never once held a leadership development session for any of my officers. After *It's Your Ship* hit the bookstores, some of my crew called me to ask, "Why didn't you tell us this stuff as you were going through it?" I was embarrassed and remorseful, and I told them so. I felt I'd let them down.

But in hindsight, I realized that I was really giving them leadership lessons all along, teaching by example. A leader's main function is to set the right example; what you do is far more important and instructive than what you say. Your true colors shine through in your actions. And if your signals don't match your words, you will not win the trust of your crew. You will certainly be leading your people by example, but you'll be leading them in the wrong direction.

So if you want your crew to pick up trash, bend over and pick up trash yourself whenever you see it on the ground. If you want people to speak the truth, talk to them truthfully. If a CEO tells his people that it's time to cut costs, he'll lose their trust and encourage their own duplicity if he then redecorates his office. After all, he's sending a very clear signal, and you can bet it won't be lost on the people who follow his every word and deed.

Leaders have to make sure the wake they leave behind isn't so turbulent that it causes damage. In my time in the Navy, one ship on a training exercise maneuvered so violently that a sailor in a small boat in its wake hit his head against the dashboard and was killed. By the same token, I've seen leaders inadvertently leave chaos among the people in their wake. Steaming smartly in and out of San Diego harbor, we sometimes left huge wakes that tossed small boats around, knocking them off course and making the occupants ill. We kept reminding ourselves to slow down and avoid swamping yachts in nearby marinas. The challenge is to chart a course and speed that knocks your adversaries off balance without destroying your allies.

Leadership is largely a matter of setting the appropriate course and speed for given conditions, and the clumsy wake is what causes the damage. Defense Secretary William Perry was highly conscious of the wake he was leaving, and careful not to cause damage by his actions. He had what I called an eight-track mind, referring to those 1970s cassette decks with all eight tracks spinning at once. In a tight situation, you could almost see Dr. Perry's tracks spinning in unison. He crafted his words with care, sending just the right message to all parties concerned with a combustible issue. Speaking to the military, for example, he chose words both patriotic yet unthreatening to potential adversaries in China or Russia.

In this global media age, careless remarks can ricochet around the world in hours or even minutes, causing large wakes in some countries and barely ripples in others. Sometimes, you may want to create that large wake. But whatever your purpose, it's essential to plan the desired effect in advance, doing your best to avoid unintended consequences. Next time you watch our elected leaders delivering tone-deaf messages on global television, take a moment to imagine the adverse effect on other cultures and leaders eager to exploit that reaction. Think before you speak: This rule applies to leaders at all levels—corporations, organizations, communities, families. What we say to one group has an effect on others—and more than ever in the Internet era of instant communication.

In my twenty-seven months of Pentagon duty, I saw Dr. Perry slip up only once. Speaking to Congress and Americans in general, Perry aimed to counter a series of Navy follies and mishaps, ranging from the Tailhook scandal (pilots drunk and disorderly) to the suicide of the chief of naval operations. Perry understandably pointed out that despite these and other scandals, the United States still had "the best damn Navy in the world." His Asian track wasn't spinning. It turned out that Perry's Ameri-centric words infuriated Chinese naval officials, who interpreted them as a condescending remark.

Having absorbed that lesson, I was always conscious of how my words affected all hands and constituencies on *Benfold* and in our battle group. Even so, I find that I still make mistakes by not employing all eight tracks. For example, in *It's Your Ship*, I often mentioned that many sailors came from disadvantaged backgrounds and had joined the Navy to get away from drugs or bad situations at home. My remarks prompted complaints from many of my sailors, who didn't consider themselves disadvantaged. I was literally stunned at the response, but I shouldn't have been surprised.

I myself came from what today would be considered a lower-middle-class family. My parents, a teacher and a social worker, supported themselves and their seven children on modest paychecks. To save money, we bought only used cars. There was no spare cash. But looking back, I can't say that I was disadvantaged. Nor should I have implied that many people in the military were. I left a sloppy wake and offended a group of people for whom I have the utmost respect and admiration. Lesson learned.

Nothing much seems to have changed in the decades since I studied at Annapolis. Not long ago, the academy was wringing its hands over excessive drinking by students, a serious problem on college campuses today. But rather than crack down on the young men and women who were actually getting drunk and into trouble, any midshipman suspected of drinking is forced to undergo a Breathalyzer test, even if he or she has done nothing wrong.

Treating midshipmen as guilty until proven otherwise is a demeaning policy. Young men and women who are learning to be naval officers should not be treated as criminals for no reason; such unsubstantiated attacks on a person's character are not conducive to building leadership skills. Worse yet, anyone who flunks the Breathalyzer test can be disciplined so severely that midshipmen who don't really know if they have stepped over the line stay out all night anyway. They reason that it is better to get a lesser punishment for unauthorized absence than to risk possible expulsion from the academy for failing a Breathalyzer test.

When the academy got a new superintendent, he turned out to have a nostalgic yearning for "the way things used to be." Over the years, more and more students had begun taking their meals at outside establishments instead of eating together in the mess hall as in former times.

The new superintendent, seeking to make the academy more like it had been in his own student days, ordered all midshipmen to eat in the mess hall. His explanation was that he wanted to create more unity and cohesion. That was perfectly understandable and laudable. But someone forgot to tell the supply officer to budget for extra food.

Soon the mess hall was running out of food at every meal. Midshipmen were going hungry and parents were organizing care packages and food caravans. The *Baltimore Sun*, which seems to have an ongoing feud with the academy, dug out the story and gleefully recounted it. The account included the commandant's explanation that the shortage was nothing more than a short-term by-product of "overhauling the menu," which had attracted more people to the mess hall. Her explanation for the newspaper's readers sent a different signal to 4,600 midshipmen, all of whom knew the real story. The net result was more cynicism and a lesson for midshipmen in the ancient art of butt-covering. None of it was a shining example of leadership.

Poor leadership produces mixed signals, which in turn confuse and demoralize the crew. An example can be found in most, if not all, national retail chains. If you visit several different stores, you're likely to find glaring differences—no matter what the chain's stated policies and training exercises might dictate. Some stores will be more welcoming, more eager to help the customer, and sharper in every measure of service. Why the discrepancies from one location to the next? It's the signals sent by store managers. A manager who is positive and optimistic and upbeat with customers will send that message to her people. If a manager is dour and pessimistic, her staff will also follow her lead.

So a leader must be on her toes to make sure she is sending the right signals to her crew. Even an inadvertent slipup can confuse employees and possibly disenchant them about the quality of your leadership. But if you strive to maintain an honest relationship and good rapport with your staff, mistakes can be rectified and confidence regained. At the end of the day, it is the strength of your example that will allow you to lead with success and create new leaders in your own image. What follows are some hard-earned lessons in leadership with courage that will help you achieve your goals.

LEADERS CAN BE FOUND SWABBING THE DECK.

Leadership isn't reserved only for those who are anointed from on high. Leaders can lurk in unexpected places. As we saw in Chapter 2 regarding the bombing of the London Underground, frontline troops in good organizations know how to lead.

And leadership from the front isn't reserved for times of crisis. How many people know their bank tellers? After I got out of the Navy, I went to my local SunTrust branch to set up a new checking account. The teller, Kim Elliot, was one of the most engaging women I've ever worked with. If there were no customer lines, we would talk for maybe ten or fifteen minutes.

During one of our conversations, she asked what I did, and when I told her, she offered me the benefits of a small business account. I took her advice and opened one. Later, when I was preparing to buy a house, I sought Kim's advice again, and this time she pointed me toward a SunTrust mortgage. But besides all the great advice I got from Kim, I was struck by how just one person in a frontline, lower-paying job could generate tens of thousands of dollars in business for a bank simply by being pleasant and upbeat and taking a genuine interest in her customers. It wasn't the head of the mortgage operation who won my business; Kim was able to function like a leader and grow business for her bank just by being friendly.

It's the Kim Elliots in workplaces all across the country who are building great relationships with customers. I've been with Sun-Trust ever since Kim made me feel like a special customer.

FAILURE CAN BE A POWERFUL LESSON.

Few people are born knowing how to lead. Most of us have to learn it just as I did, with plenty of failures along the way. Chris Major learned to be a leader in what may be the hardest way there is: He failed so completely that his disgusted crew confronted him with his faults and missteps. After that, against all odds, Chris bootstrapped himself to the top of the leadership class.

Chris is a firefighter, a lieutenant in Colorado's Parker Fire District, based about twenty miles southeast of Denver. He had been a standout soldier who was promoted to sergeant at a very young age in the U.S. Army, a feat not replicated as a firefighter when it took him three times testing in a very competitive process to be promoted to lieutenant in his district. He thought of himself as a student of leadership, and he read the latest books on the subject and tried out assorted techniques inspired by his reading.

Chris, whose firehouse nickname was Dawg, also thought he was beloved as well as successful. His first assignment as lieutenant, leading a three-man crew of seasoned professionals, had gone without a hitch. But as the crew expanded and took in newer firefighters, Chris unintentionally reverted to habits he had learned in the military. He began to display a top-down, command-and-control, my-way-or-the-highway attitude. He belittled people for lack of knowledge and berated them for doing things any way but his. He was often grouchy, and insisted on taking the lead role in any situation.

"I had always told myself I wasn't going to do that—that it's not the right thing for the firehouse," he told me. "But I ended up falling right back into the military ways. I went through a transformation for some reason. I really don't know why." Crew member Brian Netzel said Chris's transformations typically occurred after he had experimented with some new leadership technique. Then, after a week or a month of trying a new method, Chris would revert to being "the same ol' Dawg again." And the affection Chris thought he felt from his men was beginning to evaporate.

Finally, his six firefighters got their fill of Chris's bullying attitude. They set up a meeting and, one by one, read him his list of sins. Chris heard them out, and he interpreted their message as: "You're really screwing up the way you're leading us. We're all going to put in for a transfer."

Anger, betrayal, shock, remorse: Chris felt them all. These were the men he lived with in the firehouse. They had his back and he had theirs—or so he had thought until that moment of unvarnished truth. Here they were, telling him they could barely stand him. And seeking transfers? No one requested to be transferred out of a station unless he wanted specific training that wasn't available within the unit. But now, six capable firefighters were willing to transfer just to escape being under the thumb of one lousy boss, Chris Major. That kind of hard-hitting message will get a leader's attention.

After the men vented their frustrations, the battalion chief meted out Chris's penance: He was to read one more book about leadership: *It's Your Ship*. And now Chris was ready to heed the advice.

All any of us needs to make a positive change in our lives is one serendipitous moment that forces us to look at the world with new eyes. Chris had gained that new perspective.

After the confrontation, Chris vowed that, despite all his previous failed attempts to change, this time would be different. He would dial back the pressure he was putting on young and less-experienced firefighters. He would start listening again. He would let others try their hand at leadership.

And he did exactly what he promised. There's been no backsliding, reported Brian, who added: "He always knew what it took to be a good leader; he just didn't follow his own rules. And now I think he's following those rules."

CURE THE HEAVY-BADGE SYNDROME.

Chris's big breakthrough was his realization that his rigid and controlling manner dated back to his Army days. When he made sergeant at such an early age, it was a challenge to supervise a large number of people, many of whom were older than Chris. "I felt if I didn't show dominance right away, they were going to walk all over me," he told me. "I guess some of the same feelings reappeared at the fire station after I made lieutenant—like, I made it this far and nobody's going to get in the way. It was sort of the heavy-badge syndrome."

Master Chief Scheeler confessed to having much the same attitude earlier in his Navy career. As a chief petty officer, "I was probably far more vocal than I needed to be," he told me. "There was some 'do as I say, not as I do,' but I was also one of those types who'd rip a kid's face off in a New York minute." Of course, when Scheeler was a young sailor, chiefs were mean, foul people. "If you had to go see the chief," he said, "it was because all else had failed, and the first thing he was going to do was to rip into you for either not performing well on the beach or not performing well at work."

Not surprisingly, Scheeler imitated what he'd seen. "I viewed all the people assigned to me as mine, as much mine as my assigned equipment," he recalled. "So my view of the world at that time was that it was okay for me to lead and guide and discipline, and I did a lot of discipline, a lot of heavy-handed discipline." The master chief said that "my guys clearly knew what my standards were and what my thresholds were, but they also knew that no matter what—right, wrong, or indifferent—I was their chief defender, their chief champion, the chief mentor. . . . I protected them as if they were my own children. What I didn't realize is that they weren't my children. They were young men serving their country who needed a bit more of gentle guidance and a lot less of an iron fist."

Bob Scheeler's big breakthrough came when, as command master chief, he was tasked with developing *Benfold*'s cadre of chief petty officers. He told me he desperately wanted his chiefs to be viewed not as the ogres of old, but as "people their personnel could turn to in time of need, people who would lead them by example, either technically, or personally, or professionally."

After Chris Major had his epiphany, he made major changes. No longer were his ideas cookie-cutter strategies copied from a how-to book or a Web site. Instead, the things he tried flowed from his own view of the world and his understanding of the men and women he wished to lead. He looked at his team as individuals and saw his goals in terms of the winning ways that would make those goals reachable.

"Probably the biggest thing for me was realizing that these are smart people who have brains, and I can't always be in control, and that I'm there in a support role." Chris rattled off his healthy new views as if they had come to him in one crystal-clear moment. But that wasn't the case. "It was really difficult that first month to step back," he said. "I had to restrain myself in the front seat of the fire truck on a fire alarm, just to make sure I'd let the crew go in and run it."

Unsure that this new Dawg was for real, Chris's crew felt confused at first. They weren't sure he was really changing. And Chris understands why: "Over and over and over, I had showed them what to do, and usually for the same types of calls. A lot of the time, they were going to do it on their own just as I wanted them to without me having to say anything, and I was just jumping the gun. Now I stopped and let them do it themselves." It was exactly what Chris's team had wanted, but it was still disconcerting to have him finally step aside and let them do their jobs.

DON'T HOLD YOUR PEOPLE DOWN.

When I talked to Chris about his managerial makeover, I asked if he had encountered any particular sticking points along the way. I had to laugh when he answered, "the radio."

I myself had kept a tight grip on *Benfold*'s radio and set strict standards for any crew member authorized to use it. I wanted to make sure that no one said anything that might sound inappropriate or incompetent to a commodore or admiral who might be listening in.

All leaders have certain tools or tokens that represent power, things we are reluctant to let go of. For Chris and me, the communication system was an instrument of power. Chris was used to being in control of his unit's radio, dictating what could and could not be said, when, and by whom. But as he gained confidence in his crew's ability to function independently, he was able to toss this crutch aside.

Like me when I learned to relax, Chris began to wonder just what was so scary about letting the lower ranks speak and be heard. "I realized that it's not going to hurt anybody if they don't say exactly what I would say on the radio, and, frankly, what I would say is not always right. Yes, they sometimes make mistakes, but they learn that way, and it's not a big deal."

By hanging back and bringing up the rear, Chris has found opportunities to be a better teacher and mentor to his crew. When his leadership largely consisted of doing the job himself or giving his men step-by-step orders, Chris could see the problem and the solution from only one angle: his. He never widened his view to take in the thoughts, skills, and solutions of his firefighters. From his new vantage point, he's able to watch, consider, and make better judgments.

Chris sums up the lessons he has learned in a simple fashion: "Give people a chance to succeed, and they will do so beyond your wildest dreams." His crew "always had the skills," he told me, "but they were being held down." Now that he has freed them to use their skills, excellence is bursting out all over. "Two of my guys are probably top candidates for the next promotional exam to lieutenant," he reported proudly. As it happens, they were also part of the gutsy bunch who first told Chris he had to make some changes.

In my experience, leaders who constantly proclaim that "people are our most valued asset" frequently don't value anyone. To lead by example, you must be clear about how to treat your people and how to set them up to succeed. On *Benfold*, everything I did as captain was for the ship and the crew, and I intentionally did things to show them that it wasn't about me. I never redecorated my captain's cabin, for example, or set the crew to pointless work to make me look good. It was all about making sure that our people had the best training, the best facilities, and the most opportunities to achieve their personal best.

EMBRACE THE POWER—AND PLEASURE—
OF PANACHE.

My first real lesson in leadership style came from my mentor on *Albert David*. His name was Steve McLaughlin and he was the navigator. Steve, who reminded me of the title character in *Crocodile Dundee*, a popular movie back in the day, was a big, charismatic guy, an outdoorsman who won followers by doing everything with panache. Like the eccentric Aussie film character he resembled, he even sang "Waltzing Matilda." He was clearly the best junior officer on that ship, and he was the one who took me under his wing, helped me get my sea legs, and taught me how to drive the ship.

Steve also taught me how to refuel our ship from an oiler. Refueling at sea is a very scary maneuver, especially in heavy seas. The ship handler has to come alongside the tanker, separated by 120 feet of angry water. Booms hold the refueling line between the ships. The line can snap if the ships diverge, or it can drag in the water and break if the ships get too close. It's a harrowing job, to say the least. As with everything else, though, Steve performed the feat with confidence and dash, and I was eager to emulate him.

After Steve left *Albert David*, the captain nominated me for the annual ship-handling competition. We were in the western Pacific, and the squadron commander was going from ship to ship evaluating the junior officers on coming into port, refueling, and several other complex maneuvers. In the refueling exercise, we were 4,000 yards ahead of the oiler and were ordered to take a waiting station 1,000 yards off its stern.

The challenge was to drop off to one side, slow down, and then pick the exact moment to come in fast, dead astern of the oiler, making allowance for the relative speed of the two ships, the wind, the current, and the effect of the waves. There were no charts to follow. We simply had to put our rudder over and sense how fast we needed to go.

It's a seat-of-the-pants maneuver, and you can't be slow or tentative. It's a little like a hockey player making a flashy, curving stop to be in perfect position for a slap shot—very tricky. Sometimes ships will hit the oiler dead-on if the skipper misjudges.

Well, I did it at full power, twenty-seven knots on that ship. I was using my seaman's eye, a sense of judgment that I had learned from Steve, and I took station in perfect position. I have to admit that a little luck was involved, but it was a big-league performance, and I won the award for our squadron. When the commander in chief of the Pacific Fleet announced the winners, I was the only ensign on the list. Most of them were lieutenants or lieutenant commanders.

A CHALLENGE FROM THE BLUE SETS HEADS TO THINKING.

Learning to depend on a seaman's eye was a lesson I wanted to pass along to the young officers on *Benfold*. I got the chance one day on the way to Singapore, when we were traveling again with *Gary* and *Harry W. Hill*.

I came up to the bridge from lunch to find Elliot Avidan, one of my lieutenants, driving the ship. He was a promising young officer, but he didn't have a lot of confidence or any instinctive talent for handling the ship.

On the spur of the moment, I told Elliot to cut over and take station 1,000 yards behind *Gary*. He got out his maneuvering board and started to figure the mathematics of how far to turn the rudder and what speed would be needed. I barked, "Elliot, just drive the ship and go take station astern." He still didn't understand that I wanted him to drive by seaman's eye. But reluctantly, he put the rudder over and increased speed, and after a couple of zigzags, we settled into station 1,000 yards astern of *Gary*. Then I told him to put *Benfold* 1,000 yards astern of *Harry W. Hill*. By this time, Elliot was getting the hang of it, and he did a pretty good job.

He was also having fun. Because the challenge was unplanned and totally unexpected, it had an element of suspense, excitement, and risk that broke the monotony of the routine watch. In fact, the challenge worked out so well that several times that day I did it again, ordering the conning officer to toggle back and forth between the two destroyers.

Of course, word traveled fast, so all the officers of the deck started mentally rehearsing how they'd take the assigned stations if I suddenly gave the order. That planning helped give them the courage and confidence to do it, and with actual practice, all of them started developing their seamen's eyes. I got more skilled ship handlers as a result.

Even better, my challenge forced the men to start developing the same mind-set for all the other challenges they might face. They began to imagine scenarios and figure out a way to react to them, and I encouraged that in every way I knew. They were beginning to be real naval officers, on their way to the responsibility of command. Shouldn't occasional surprise challenges be a tool for business leaders to help sharpen their people's agility in a crisis? What better way to build company-wide confidence, skill, and (no coincidence) your bottom line?

DEFINE YOUR FIELD OF PLAY.

A large part of leadership is simply figuring out your field of operation. In Chapter 1, I confessed the mistake I made in thinking of "your ship" instead of "our ship"; I was focusing too much on *Benfold* and not enough on the rest of my battle group. When I tell that story, people sometimes ask me, "Why stop there?" Shouldn't the term "our ship" have included the whole Pacific Fleet, even the whole United States Navy?

My answer is no, because that would be biting off more than one captain and crew could chew. You have to focus on what you can control. I couldn't change the whole Navy, and I would have been fired if I had tried. But I could try to influence the part of the Navy in which I was operating.

Where I made my mistake was in thinking too small about what that territory included. I should have realized that *Benfold* would succeed only as part of its battle group, and also that I didn't have a monopoly on great ideas. There might have been other ships out there doing things I had never thought of and wouldn't hear about because we didn't have a forum for exchanging that information.

So what I should have done was to talk to the battle group commander privately and ask him, "Why don't you force the ten of us to work better together? Why don't we start a program so every week or two we have lunch on one of the ships, all ten captains, where we can close the door and talk about our issues and share best practices?" But I wasn't smart enough to figure that out at the time.

It's never easy to see things from a new perspective, as I have learned over and over in my career. As just one example, I have to admit I was a little disappointed when I first met my executive officer on *Benfold*. Jeff Harley seemed mild-mannered and almost professorial, hardly the typical model of a hard-charging Navy officer. And I was more than a little insecure about taking over *Benfold*. I knew that I was going to need a great second in command to help me. If I'd had any say in the matter, I would have picked almost anyone else. Luckily, I had no choice of XOs, and in short order, I was in awe of Jeff's knowledge and skills. And for what it's worth, I completely misjudged his personality. He was one of the best officers I ever served with, and I learned a lot from him. He gained not only my respect and confidence but that of the crew as well.

I did what I thought was a small thing for Jeff, and it cemented our relationship for good. It turned out that my predecessor had never let Jeff sit in the XO's chair on the bridge. I told him it was his.

There are two chairs in the pilot house, big leather reclining chairs on four-foot pedestals. The right-hand chair is for the captain and the left-hand one is for the XO, unless the commodore or admiral is onboard; in that case, the visiting brass gets the XO's chair. Everyone else on the bridge has to stand all the time. They're good chairs to sit in, but they're also a symbol that these guys are in command.

When I gave Jeff the right to sit in his chair, I thought I was just redressing a petty injustice. But it turned out that I was redefining his field of play. The chair meant so much to him that he would get up early and go up to the bridge to sit there and watch the sun rise. Jeff later became commanding officer of USS *Milius* and was superb. He is truly a remarkable leader.

REHEARSE THE WHAT-IF SCENARIOS.

Effective leadership demands that you be prepared for unpleasant surprises, which are never in short supply. That's one thing the Naval Academy did teach me.

I started thinking about what-if scenarios after a series of Vietnam veterans who had been prisoners of war—John McCain, Jeremiah Denton, Richard Stratton, and Vice Admiral James Stockdale—came to Annapolis to tell their stories. Vice Admiral Stockdale had been the senior ranking officer in the prison where he was held. He told us that he used to bang his head against the wall before being photographed, so that in case he broke under torture, people would see blood streaming down his face and understand that he had been forced to betray his country.

I asked myself if I would have that kind of courage and moral strength should I ever find myself in a similar situation. At the time, I knew I didn't have it, and I didn't know how I was going to build such interior strength. Still, I thought that if I could prepare myself ahead of time, I might be able to handle challenges better.

That kind of thinking taught me to consider the things that could go wrong. On *Benfold*, I would sit on the bridge or lie in my bunk picturing all the what-if scenarios, and figuring out what to do about them and how to train the crew for the situation.

Preparing what-if scenarios has been standard practice in the Navy for decades. Before any exercise, everyone involved gets together for a briefing to rehearse the expected action and prepare for contingencies. On *Benfold*, we went several steps further. If we were going to shoot the guns, for instance, the safety officers would brief everyone on the sequence of procedures, the precautions to prevent shooting at anything but the target, what would be done if there were a misfire, how to handle an accident, and the preparations for medical contingencies. Everyone who had a role in the exercise had to cover the major possible scenarios and show that they were prepared for all of them, with safeguards in place if something went wrong.

Bill Walsh went through what-if exercises time and again as coach of the San Francisco 49ers. If the team won by thirty-nine points, he said once, "I would wake up in the middle of the night and see how we could have won by forty-two." He would imagine how his next rival might plot to nullify a 49er play, and have his players practice how to counter that hypothetical ploy so they would not be surprised if it actually happened. Standing on the sideline during the game, Walsh was serene in the knowledge that he had every option covered; the 49ers never panicked.

LOVE WHAT YOU DO.

In his role as chief petty officer, my old friend Darren Barton spends a lot of his time trying to instill initiative in new recruits to the Navy and persuading them to make the effort to be their best. Sometimes, he told me not long ago, the recruits resent their new life and feel they're getting the short end of the stick. Darren tells them they're just in a bad patch, that the Navy offers a great life with a great benefits package, and that the light at the end of the tunnel is not an oncoming train.

Some get it and others don't, Darren said, but his strongest and most effective message is sent by his own attitude. "I love what I do," he says simply. "This is the best job I've ever done." Working for the Navy is a joy to him; "Crazy as it may sound, I even love being out at sea." That message is conveyed in his body language and everything he does, and it gets through to all but the most stubborn recruits.

Darren also sets an example of leadership for the other petty officers. One of them, he told me, would get angry and abusive when sailors shirked their jobs or didn't do them correctly. "It seemed that yelling was his main style," Darren said. "I had to sit him down and tell him that he was wasting a lot of energy, and there was another way to handle it."

Sometimes, he went on, sailors just don't understand what they are supposed to do. He told his colleague to talk to them, show a little more patience, and see what happens. The petty officer heard the message and followed Darren's advice. And sure enough, the errant sailors understood his patient explanations and did better at their jobs.

BE OUT IN FRONT.

If something is going to happen anyway, get out in front and lead it.

I did it myself on the issue of Friday afternoon liberty for the crew of *Benfold*. It became obvious that the chief petty officers were quietly giving some of the crew permission to get an early start on their weekends in port by taking Friday afternoons off. It was part of the chiefs' system of rewards and punishments, and it wasn't doing any damage. But the sailors were slinking away, trying not to let the officers see them leaving the ship.

I decided I would give Friday afternoon liberty to everyone who wasn't on weekend watch if the ship was cleaned and the maintenance done. It was happening anyway, but I got the credit. The reaction was, "Hey, the captain is giving us Friday afternoon off."

So instead of the crew feeling like they had to sneak off the ship, they now left with heads held high for having gotten all of their work done efficiently. By the way, I usually left the ship about five minutes before they did. The captain of *Benfold* led the early-weekend parade down the pier. The crew couldn't have been happier.

JUST DO THE RIGHT THING.

Most leadership rules are flexible and contingent. Like our rights under the Constitution, they can all be trumped by other rules, depending on the circumstances. But there's one principle that I have found as constant as the Pole Star, good in all weather and never to be broken. In a Machiavellian world it sounds naive and almost childish, but genuine leaders know it and live by it: Do the right thing.

There are times when there is no right thing to do and you have to choose the least bad alternative. But in most cases, it's clear which course will be the moral, ethical, honorable choice. That's what you should do, and you do it.

I know no better illustration of this precept than the crisis that enveloped Baxter International in the summer of 2001, after elderly patients in Spanish hospitals began dying suddenly and painfully at an alarming rate. Health officials traced the cause to faulty dialysis filters manufactured by Sweden's Althin Medical Lab, a recent Baxter acquisition. Soon the toll mounted to fifty-three deaths in six countries, including the United States.

Baxter is a $7.7 billion maker of medical products for patients with life-threatening diseases. Its CEO, Harry M. Jansen Kraemer Jr., was facing a problem familiar to many leaders: how to deal with a crisis and at the same time protect his company's reputation for honesty and integrity. Baxter quickly recalled the specific lot of Althin dialysis filters linked to the Spanish deaths. Two scientific analyses found nothing wrong with the filters, and the company saw no reason to accept further responsibility.

But then came shocking news from Croatia: Twenty-three dialysis patients had died at clinics across that country. Officials now blamed Baxter, which promptly ordered a global recall of all Althin filters and mobilized its best medical investigators to find answers. The experts remained stumped for weeks.

Then one day a quality engineer at Althin's Swedish plant noticed a few liquid bubbles on one of the recalled filters. The liquid was a 3M chemical used to test for air leaks in the filters. It was chemically nontoxic, and it was supposed to be vacuumed away before shipping. But somehow the chemical had remained on some filters in certain Althin lots. Tests on rabbits soon showed that the substance became toxic when heated to body temperature in a patient's bloodstream. Result: a fatal pulmonary embolism.

Upon receiving this bulletin, Baxter's CEO had just one comment: "Let's make sure we do the right thing." Harry Kraemer could easily have ducked, quietly pulling the filters (a mere $20 million revenue stream) off the market and dumping the blame on Althin's previous owners, on 3M, or on assorted officials in Croatia and Spain who had stonewalled the initial probe.

But Kraemer didn't deny, shirk, or spin. He immediately went public with a detailed report on the company's findings. Not only that: The company shut down Althin for good, took a $189 million charge to earnings to cover the closure, and began settling with families of the dead patients. Baxter also spent the next year reviewing and improving its manufacturing processes worldwide.

And by the way, Kraemer urged Baxter's directors to cut his 2001 performance bonus by at least 40 percent and those of his top executives by 20 percent. Death and disaster had occurred on their watch, he said. They were responsible.

Asked later how Baxter would now handle future crises, Kraemer looked a bit surprised. "Of course we'll do the right thing," he said. "As opposed to what?"

It had been a costly misadventure, cutting well over $200 million from Baxter's bottom line. But unlike some other pharmaceutical companies with similar problems, Baxter emerged with its integrity not just intact but enhanced. It was recently named by the Ethisphere Council as one of the 100 World's Most Ethical Companies. As for Harry Kraemer, he was widely praised in the business press and went on to become executive partner at the private equity firm of Madison Dearborn Partners and a professor at Northwestern University's Kellogg School of Management. I can only hope his students will follow his example.

Poor leadership is, unfortunately, not in short supply in organizations. There's ample proof of that in today's headlines about money squandered, opportunity lost, contracts bungled, risks mismanaged, and employees losing their jobs. But there are still plenty of leaders who are striving every day to do the right thing and to inspire their own people to emulate their winning ways. My hope is that the lessons you've gleaned from the inspirational leaders in these pages will serve you well and help turn your company into a leadership engine.

Epilogue

In a memorable speech, the famed business leader and author Lawrence Bossidy once summed up the American psyche: "We're a freedom-loving people, an entrepreneurial, democratic people. Americans don't like to be managed, or treated like children. They want to be asked for their ideas. They want to work in meritocracies where accountability is high and the best people get ahead. They want to be communicated with frequently about how the organization is performing. They want to broaden their skill base. They want to have a chance to own a stake in the companies for which they work."

Responding to these impulses is the key to revitalizing life and work in the America of our time. Organizations of all kinds, private and public, need leaders able and willing to summon the country's best instincts, beginning with their own.

Imagine a world of great crews manning great ships—a new century of brilliant captains and intrepid sailors, joined as brothers and sisters in taking big risks and taming wild storms, human as well as natural.

Am I dreaming? Hardly. After years of studying leadership across America, I wrote this book to tell you and thousands of others that the arts of persuading ordinary people to work together in extraordinary ways have never been more effective.

The stories I offer here begin with my own comeuppance. Inordinately proud of skippering the best ship in the U.S. Navy, I discovered that leaders without humility are like apples without cores: seedless and sterile. Nearly all organizations pulsing with life owe it to some empathetic leader given to looking not into mirrors but into other people's faces and feelings. He or she knows a secret: Never pit your people against each other in a ruthless competition. Teach collaboration, the liberating power of disparate people uniting their talents for a common purpose.

Collaboration is probably the key word in this book. It's the leader's tool for making an organization unbeatable. But other adjectives that flag a successful leader's most important traits include welcoming, inspiring, trusting, expecting, risking, empowering, delegating, praising, *freeing*, and *encouraging*.

The last two apply in particular to what great leaders do for everyone around them, whether subordinates or superiors. They give off heat, an energy that frees others of their inhibitions and encourages people to start controlling their own destinies. That's what I hope this book itself will do for you—as it has already for me.

Acknowledgments

I would like to acknowledge and thank the wonderful men and women in the military, National Guard, and the Reserves, who sacrifice so much to keep our country strong and free. The sacrifices they and their families make are considerable, and we as a nation don't do nearly enough to thank them for their dedication and selflessness. I would also like to recognize our first responders—our police, firefighters, and EMTs—who also serve their country and communities with distinction.

I have been blessed my entire adult life working with many wonderful people. The crew of USS *Benfold* were phenomenal and my respect for them knows no bounds. Since leaving the Navy, I have also had the great pleasure of working with the wonderful people at the Washington Speakers Bureau, who represent me with distinction and class. Bernie Swain, Harry Rhoades, and Tony D'Amelio are the best in the business.

I am also blessed to have a wonderful literary agent, Helen Rees. She is a great friend and mentor and has always given me the best advice and guidance. I also work with the best writing team ever assembled. Donna Carpenter and Mo Coyle are true professionals and friends and we have become a great team.

Finally, I would like to recognize my mother, Mary Margaret, who is a wonderful role model and matriarch of the extended Abrashoff clan.

On the editorial side, I'd like to take a moment to sincerely thank the good people at Grand Central Publishing. Rick Wolff, my editor, first signed me on with *It's Your Ship*, and that book has sailed smoothly for many years on all the best-seller lists. And when Rick approached me with this natural sequel, *It's Our Ship*, I immediately felt we had another winner onboard. I also want to thank Rick's hardworking colleagues, especially Mari Okuda, Bob Castillo, Harvey-Jane Kowal, Karen Thompson, Tracy Martin, and Ann McCarthy, for all of their outstanding contributions.